WOMEN STRUGGLE FOR SUSTAINABILITY

WOMEN STRUGGLE FOR SUSTAINABILITY

SIDDHARTHA SARKAR
Department of Commerce
Dinhata College, Dinhata,
Cooch Behar, West Bengal, India

SERIALS PUBLICATIONS
NEW DELHI

First Published - 2006

ISBN: 81-8387-040-6

Published by

SERIALS PUBLICATIONS
4830/24, Prahlad Street, Ansari Road
Darya Ganj, New Delhi-110002 (India)
Phone : 23245225
Fax : 91-11-23272135
E-mail: serials@satyam.net.in

Contents

Contents

Prologue

The vulnerable women suffer from the larger level of bribes than the non-poor households. With the difficult economic conditions of transition, a number of women no longer value edification as much as they did before the transition; their pinnacle priority is mere survival. In most ethnicity, women and men have differing roles and responsibilities according to socially defined division of labour based on gender. This gender inequity is reflected in a variety of social and economic dimensions. In terms of reproductive activities, women generally have primary responsibility for the care and feeding of children and families, as well as health care and education. In many developing countries, it is the women who perform most of the work related to subsistence agriculture, plus gathering and managing fuel and water as a part of the household responsibility. Their productive activities are often unpaid and labour-intensive. When women in rural areas do generate income, it tends to be within the informal sector, and not adequately reflected in national accounting systems. This serves to under-represent the importance of energy as an input to women's economic activities. Because they operate mostly in the informal and unpaid sectors, poor women have less access to financial resources, credit and equipment than do men, and less of a voice in household, or community-level, decision making. Gender-poverty is a problem that has a disproportionate effect on women and girls, especially in rural areas. The most obvious factors relate to time and physical effort. Many women in developing countries have to spend long hours gathering fuel and hauling water, using their own labour to carry heavy loads over long distances in addition to other informal work. When women are overburdened, they are more likely to keep their daughters home from school to assist with own household activities, including fuel and water collection, thereby limiting opportunities for girls to move forward through education, and rising the likelihood that their families will remain in poverty.

This book examines women's link to socioeconomic development and offers guidance on how informal activities can become important instruments for eliminating poverty, regenerating the environment, creating employment opportunities, promoting sustainable livelihoods, and advancing the status of women. The book looks at critical policy and programme design options to improve women's access to economic activities for sustainable development.

The author would like to extend his gratitude to several individuals especially Prof. N. Narayana of University of Botswana, Botswana, Prof. Chem Tisdell of University of Queensland, Australia and Prof. Kishore G. Kulkarni of Metropolitan State College of Denver, USA for the thriving completion of the present study.

Dr. Siddhartha Sarkar

Chapter - 1

Women and Informality

INTRODUCTION

The term informal sector and informal economy are used interchangeably to refer to that segment of the economy and labour market, which has absorbed significant numbers of job seekers and unemployed workers outside government regulations and formal systems of labour and social protection. The informal sector is becoming gradually recognized as an imperative segments of the labour market in many countries, especially developing and transition countries and thus plays a major role in employment creation, production and income generation. Research efforts in urban employment and urban labour markets have most often focused on the formal sector with an emphasis on industrial employment (Mehta 1995: 326). In countries with high rates of population growth and/or urbanization, the informal sector tends to absorb most of the growing labour force in the urban areas. Informal sector employment is a necessary survival strategy in countries that lack social safety nets such as unemployment insurance or where wages, especially in the public sector are low. In such situation, indicators such as unemployment rates and time related underemployment are not sufficient to portray the labour market situation. In other countries, the process of industrial restructuring in the formal sector is seen as leading to a greater decentralization of production through subcontracting to tiny enterprises, many of which are in the informal sector (Hussmanns 1998).

Starting from complete ignore, then phenomenon of informal economic activity has grown to be a subject of study by many researchers, both governmental and non-governmental. The nature and the means of the informal economy changed with the deregulation and liberalization while rules of competition were being set up. Informal labour obviously represents only a part of the underground or hidden or shadow or informal sector. Underground employment or informal labour may be defined as additional or primary job, which is performed through by passing regulations of the labour or tax system. Such a definition can be applied to both illegal employment between households and enterprises, irrespective of whether they are registered or not, and it also covers self-employment. This definition may also apply to outsiders and to work, which is not paid for. Informal labour can be grouped or classified according to various criteria. It may represent the principal or the additional place of employment. Underground employment may be permanent or temporary. As far as the economic sectors are concerned, illegal employment may be found in industry, construction, agriculture, transportation and services. Illegal employment may be provided by residents and non-residents of a country. The essence of an informal economy is to escape from being measured and captured, therefore both definition and methodologies shall be treated only as a way of approximation more than elsewhere in the economy in general. The informal economy is particularly flexible in reacting to changes in the regulatory framework, every groundbreaking prohibition or regulation widens its scope and size.

Though the term informal sector has been used to describe a set of economic activities that take place outside the recognized institutional framework it calls for some further elaboration and clarification. All enterprises operating on own account as well as most of the micro enterprises are assumed to fall outside the recognized institutional framework and hence belong to the informal part of the economy or simply the informal sector. It is obvious that the institutional framework is but a criterion by which the enterprises are classified into formal and informal. Redefining this criterion will no doubt affect the relative magnitudes of the two segments in an economy. But it is unlikely to influence the extent of informal employment because the fundamental causes that contribute to informality in these enterprises have not been misrepresented. It is therefore clear that the institutional framework is only a criterion by which the employment quality is reviewed, it is not by itself the cause of inferior quality. This raises the question concerning what factors contribute to informality in these enterprises? Study on the informal sector worldwide during the last three decades points out that the distinguish characteristic of these enterprises is that they operate in a different business environment than the firms in the formal sector. Fundamentally they lack free access to factor and product markets, public resources, information and opportunities as the formal enterprises carry out. Consequently they opt to operate in an informal manner, avoiding compliance with most regulations. Not only they perceive diminutive benefit from compliance, more significantly full compliance adds to the cost of running an enterprise. Lack of access to resources, markets and opportunities is in part the result of non-recognition of these enterprises by the authorities concerned. Without formal recognition few enterprises can anticipate to obtain either credit from the formal financial institutions or access to proper premises and infrastructure. It is difficult to articulate which comes first whether the lack of access to resources and markets forces these enterprises to operate outside the regulation or whether non-compliance with regulations limits their access. A self employed unit operating in an unauthorized location within the country cannot obtain legal recognition until it moves into a proper location and without recognition, it cannot expect to get a proper location from the appropriate authorities which controls the allocation of space. Similarly without adequate economic means it cannot obtain a business license and without such a license, it cannot apply for a loan. But it is clear that both lack of access and non-recognition contributes to informality. To the extent lack of legal recognition is the limiting factor, clearly modifying the institutional framework to broaden such recognition can help these enterprises by improving their access to resources and markets. It can thus contribute to a reduction in informality. But it cannot eliminate it completely. This is because there are also other factors, which contribute to informality. It is supposed that there exists an institutional bias against the vulnerable and the illiterate, who are disproportionately represented in these enterprises. The markets in developing countries, besides being deficient in many respects are also supposed to be unfriendly to them. Both the regulatory and policy environment is also understood to be unfavourable for these enterprises, origins for this bias can be traced to the mistaken perception among the authorities concerned, most believe that these tiny enterprises are only marginally productive, if not unproductive. Finally, certain social and cultural factors also induce these enterprises to operate under conditions of informality because they limit their access to resources and markets. Women entrepreneurs often cannot have access to credit without the consent of men in the household or cannot work far away from residence because of family and child care responsibilities. It is this hostile environment that distinguishes these enterprises from the formal ones. It should however be noted that the formal enterprises in developing countries are also often subjected to a variety of limitations including unfavourable policy and regulatory environment and market imperfections. But the consequences to small enterprises are overwhelming in part because of their weak economic base. Informality will persist as long as these enterprises are not fully integrated with the mainstream, i.e., the institutionalized part of the economy. One major consequence of not having free access to resources and markets is that few are able to improve upon their initial endowments in terms of physical and human capital and know how, by resorting to transactions in the market, they are obliged to rely on own savings from incomes that are already meagre. These enterprises, already disadvantaged because of the small scale of operation, are further handicapped by the unsupportive business environment. The net result of all this is to oblige these enterprises to function in a manner that is in striking contrast to those in the formal sector - besides being small in terms of output and employment, they are also labour intensive, use little capital and skills, they often operate without proper business premises, work long hours, work from locations vulnerable to harassment by police, remain invisible, beyond the recognized institutional framework - the visible physical characteristics derived from informality. These are the underlying causes of informal employment. They explain why productivity and incomes are low and the conditions of work are poor in these enterprises. Another consequence of informality is that some of these enterprises choose to avoid dealing with markets altogether by seeking to operate on a subcontracting basis albeit under conditions that are considered less than fair. What distinguishes them from other own account or micro enterprises is that they often have special relationships with their contractors which influence the way they conduct their business as well as their income. Since this class of enterprises is a sub-sector of the informal sector, employment in them also forms part of informal (Psacharopoulos and Tzannatos 1992). But the factors governing their income are different. Similarly some of those operating an enterprise on own account are labeled as home-based workers or home-workers if they operate on a subcontracting basis because they have their business premises within their home or residence, but they nevertheless also form part of informal employment as defined above. At the risk of over simplification it might therefore be stated that the term informal sector or economy refers to a segment of the economy where the agents of production are not only small in scale but also operate under conditions of informality. It thus encompasses all small scale economic activities carried out by individuals, either through enterprises established and operated independently on own account, or through micro enterprises with the help of hired workers. They also often engage family labour and apprentices. It should be evident from the above discussion that informality strikes different enterprises differently, because not all these enterprises are affected by various constraints to the same degree. Some are more informal than others, measured in terms of the deviation from the established norms. Evidence from countries show that the extent to which these enterprises have free access to factor and product markets, public resources, information and opportunities varies considerably across enterprises. Some enjoy better access to credit or premises while others do not. Similar observations hold regarding compliance with laws and regulations. Some comply with none of the regulations while others comply partially e.g., they may pay the market fees or local taxes but not registered or licensed. Regulatory and policy environment affect some more severely than others. These considerations suggest that even though the enterprises are all classified as informal, in reality, the extent of informality varies across enterprises. In other words the enterprises are subjected to different degrees of informality. Informal sector is thus far from homogeneous. This also means that the extent of informal employment i.e., low income and poor conditions of work varies considerably in developing countries. From the point of view of efficiency and equity, the loss of output and welfare resulting from the presence of informality should be obvious. These informal enterprises devote considerable part of their time and energy on how to overcome informality rather than on improving their business. No attempt however has been made in the literature to measure this welfare loss. This remains a challenge and belongs to the future research agenda. Based on evidence one can put forward some general propositions: Enterprises that are smaller, those headed by poor, less educated, women and recent migrants to cities are more likely to be informal (Sethuraman 1998).

Looking at the various qualitative assessments undertaken in many developing countries, informality could aggravate poverty, either directly or indirectly, through increasing inequality in the access to services and opportunities, increased vulnerability and human abuse. The informality is an important coping means when formal systems have collapsed or are under enormous stress. People recognize that informality is harmful to their standards of living and to the distribution of income in general, but in most cases they have no choice because there are no viable formal alternatives. In some cases, however, there is a perception that through informal means it may be possible to get better deals by performing on connections or just by appealing directly for the understanding of the service provider. Indeed, in countries where formal cost recovery for services has been imposed to try and reduce under the table payments, it is not clear that the poor have been made better off. Recent research has identified a number of potentially negative impacts that informal payments have had on health care, including decreased access to healthcare for women and the poor. These informal payments, however, also allow for services that the State cannot fund to continue to exist. The problem once again is not the informal payment but the under-funding of health services. The relationship between informal payments and access is complex. It may not make much difference to the poor whether high health expenditure is official or unofficial, as hindrances would be equal in both cases. Informal payments, however, make it impossible for the government to modulate health fees in order to facilitate access by the poor. Health indicators and anecdotal evidence suggest that the increase in out of pocket payments has substantially brought down the utilization of healthcare facilities. People tend to utilize these facilities only under exceptional circumstances. Moreover, many studies show that the poor have been forced to pay an increasingly larger percentage of their income on healthcare. On the other hand, the demand for informal payments may simply arise out of the need to survive. The introduction of health insurance systems also has a negative impact on access because of the large informal sector in developing countries. The poor in the informal sector do not have formal labour contracts, so no contributions are made by their employer or by themselves to the State pension funds or for healthcare benefits. The result is that these individuals are not eligible for those services and that little money is actually paid for health insurance. Principally, for those who are at the bottom of the socioeconomic ladder and those in rural areas without access to key infrastructure, such as water and sewage systems, health and healthcare conditions are worse. The role of education is very influential in preventing people from falling into poverty and informality. The link between education and poverty is similar to that between unemployment and poverty as unemployment rates fall with every additional level of education. The poor suffer from the larger level of bribes than the non-poor households. With the difficult economic conditions of transition, a number of people no longer value education as much as they did before the transition, their pinnacle priority is mere survival. The interaction between informality and social protection raises two very different issues. First, the poor tend to rely on informal means in the traditional areas of social protection, including help for the aged, the extended family, and the handicapped and for those in extreme poverty. The high demand for benefits from the State and the low level of public funds available for this purpose in many of the countries under review limit the effectiveness of social protection systems. Consequently, many people among the elderly from large families handicapped or others have been left with no other means than their own or family support. The second issue is that the high level of informal activities considerably limits the financing available for formal social protection, especially in countries, in which payroll taxes constitutes the largest source of funds for pensions and other forms of support, such as unemployment benefits. Analyzes of informal employment in social assessment and other qualitative studies have emphasized the insecurity, hard work, very long hours, extremely low wage rates and sometime hazardous working conditions. The unemployed rarely choose to become involved in informality, preferring the security of formal employment. Nevertheless, the lack of formal employment coupled with an inability to meet household needs in the absence of welfare benefits or because of the inadequacy of the available assistance, encourages people to turn to the informal economy in response. Likewise perceive the informal employment strategies of the unemployed as a part of a survival strategy, through which some individuals develop alternative ways of working in the face of the existing limited opportunities and the failure of the welfare system. Informality enables the unemployed poor to get some basic income, but what is more important, it may help them maintain a sense of self-confidence. Most individuals work in the informal sector only if they have to or if they can supplement their informal sector earnings with their unemployment benefits and the social services, such as health care, that are available with these benefits. First of all, for the vast majority, informal sector wages are very low. The more illegal the work, the higher the wages, as well as the higher risks and fines if caught. In turn high taxes depress economic activity and income stabilization, which brings us back to square one, making informality a mechanism of survival and coping, especially for the poor. Many poor people observe the lack of fair access to the legal system and the lack of security as major components of poverty. The lack of trust in the legal system and the possibility for people to have influence on it in a non-transparent way are major issues.

In India the informal sector employs more than 90 per cent of workforce, most if not all, are covered by meaningful social security schemes. The informalised workforce is unprotected labour, which imply labour that does not have any socio-economic safety. The protection that a society provides to individuals and households to ensure access to wage and working conditions in a comprehensive sense, in matters of security of employment, health care, maternity benefits, provident fund, retirement benefits, is an essential element of the safety nets that keeps working people and their families from falling into poverty (Sarkar 2004 a: 122).

The informal sector represents an important part of the economy and certainly of labour market in many countries, especially developing countries and poses a challenge to policy makers with regard to issues relating to improvement of the working condition and social protection of the workers engaged in the informal sector. In the developing economies a substantial share of employment is indeed in informal category and women in all age groups depend on the informal sector more heavily than men. Women and children are over represented in this sector in the sense that their share in the sector is higher than their share in total labor force. Most women tend to be own account workers and only a few are heads of micro enterprises. Relatively lower level of education among women, compared to men, seems to explain, in part, this gender differential in informal employment. Discrimination in the labour market also explains in part the disproportionate concentration as it limits women's access to formal and wage employment. Women also face additional constraints because of their homemaking and childcare responsibilities, which limits their participation in formal employment. Even within the informal sector more women than men seem to be in poor quality employment. The causes for participation in the informal sector can be economic and non-economic. Economic reasons are related to unemployment and an inflexible formal labour market, a declining real price of capital and the high cost of formal production. Besides, non-economic causes are concerned with a greater flexibility and satisfaction in work, a complete use of workers professional qualifications and increased leisure time. There are two groups of factors, which determine the decision to become active in the informal sector, more specifically, the structural as well as opportunity factors. The structural factors consist of financial pressure, socio-psychological pressure and institutional constraints. The opportunity factors consist of individual background, skills, education, living condition or non-individual components, environment, values, standards etc. (Sarkar 2004 b: 366).

CONCEPT

The concept of informal sector is not easy to define specifically. Most often it is defined negatively by indicating the nonexistence of characteristics that belong to formal activities, of special emphasis being labour market characteristics, security or regularity of work, better earnings, existence of non wage and long term benefits, protective legislation and union protection (Papola 1980; Banerjee 1985). Since a number of activities within the formal sector are getting informalised and private, small scale manufacturing units employing predominantly women labour is growing–the borderline becomes blurred. While earnings may still be better in the emerging formal sector, its major advantages in terms of non-wage and long term benefits, security and protection of work likely to be getting diluted (Eapen 2001: 2390). At the same time, within the informal sector itself, evidence discloses that a number of self-employment activities in the form of micro enterprises are undertaken with great ingenuity and entrepreneurial spirit and therefore have a growth potential (Rakowski 1994).

The term informal sector was first initiated by Keith Hart (1970) in a study of urban Ghana. He describes the informal sector as that part of the urban labour force, which falls outside the organized labour market. The study identified a number of incomes and employment generating activities in the un-enumerated sector of urban settlements. The workers involved in the un-enumerated sector mainly served as self-employed, as against the wageworkers in the enumerated sector. The new entrants to the urban labour market particularly migrants from rural areas were forced to work in the informal sector partly on account of lack of adequate opportunities in the formal sector and partly due to the workers' lack of skills and adequate experience required for the jobs in the formal sector. Keith Hart has used the terms, namely, informal income generating activities, unorganized sector, un-enumerated sector, self-employed individuals and urban proletariat in his study more or less alternatively and interchangeably.

The concept has been further refined by a mission of International Labour Organization (ILO) (1972), which studied the employment situation in Kenya within the framework of the World Employment Programme. The ILO employment mission to Kenya adopted the term 'informal sector' for analysing the employment situation and for working out a strategy for employment generation in Kenya. The study reveals that informal sector has the characteristics like easy entry for the new enterprises, reliance on indigenous resources, family ownership, small scale operations, unregulated and competitive markets, labour intensive technology and informally acquired skills of workers.

Mazumdar, in a World Bank paper (1975), describes informal sector as an easy entry, residual sector providing mainly services and crowded with secondary workers with low productivity and wages.

Sethuraman (1976) has defined the informal sector as consisting of small scale units engaged in the production and distribution of goods and services with the primary objectives of generating employment and income to their participants notwithstanding the constraints on capital, both physical and human.

Tokman (1976) looks at the informal sector as a self-contained sector with well-defined and significant links with the rest of the economy.

Squire (1981) defines informal sector as a sector in which wages are determined by demand and supply forces.

Papola (1981) has defined informal sector as a convenient way of designating a segment of economy having certain characteristics, which lead to unfavourable conditions for the growth of enterprises and activities operating in this segment.

Nattrass (1987) defines informal sector at the interface of formal sector, reserve army and marginal pole.

The System of National Accounts (SNA) (1993) defined the informal sector as consisting of units engaged in the production of goods or services with the primary objective of generating employment and incomes to the persons concerned. They form part of the household sector as unincorporated enterprises owned by households. They are distinguished from corporations and quasi-corporations on the basis of their legal status and the type of accounts they hold. These household enterprises do not have a legal status independently of the households or household members owning them.

The fifteenth International Conference of Labour of ILO (1993a) adopted an operational definition of the informal sector that is irrespective of the kind of workplace, the extent of fixed assets, the duration of the activity of the enterprises and its operation as a main or secondary activity. Within the household sector, the informal sector comprises of informal own-account enterprises that are single member or partnership household units that do not hire workers on a continuous basis, enterprises of informal employers are household units owned and operated by employers, singly or in partnership, which employ one or more employees on a more or less continuous basis. For operational purposes the latter may be defined in terms of either, the size of unit below a specified level of employment or non-registration of the enterprise or its employees.

Gibson and Kelly (1994) have defined informal sector as a sector that uses inferior technology. According to them, initially multiple production processes exist in informal sector but competition among informal sector units ensures survival of only the most profitable process.

According to ILO (1999) informal sector refers to activities typically at a low level of organization and technology, with the primary objective of generating employment and income. The activities are usually carried out without proper recognition from authorities and escape the attention of the administrative machinery responsible for enforcing laws and regulation.

The labour market in developing and transition countries is strikingly different from that in the developed countries. The most arresting feature of labour markets in the developing countries is its non-homogeneous character. The labour markets in these two economies diverge in its sectoral composition with the vast majority of employment being in the non-agricultural sectors in the developed countries whereas the developing countries is still predominantly agricultural. The status of the vast majority of workers in the developed countries is of wage and salary earners whereas in the developing countries there is a predominance of self-employment. This non-homogeneous character of the labour markets in developing countries also implies that the nature of employment and the manner in which it is created is different in the two economies. Almost all the employment in developed economies is created within the recognized institutional framework as the economic agents, which create these jobs, operate within the existing laws and regulation (Sethuraman 1998). These economic agents are the government, and private enterprises, including non-corporate entities, and the employment thus created is governed by the prevailing labour laws and regulations. In contrast, in the developing countries the vast majority of the population is left to fend for itself and create employment out of its own ingenuity, skills and capital. This leads to vast differences in the nature of employment and the creation of a dualistic structure of formal and informal components of the labour market. The standard textbook model assumes a homogeneous market with an inelastic supply of labour, where demand conditions alone determine the price of labour or wage. This assumption leads to thinking about an average productivity of labour for the economy as a whole. Labour market policies based on this assumption can be quite misleading if prescribed for the developing countries. The productivity differences between the various sectors of the labour market in the developing countries are of major importance for both labour market outcomes and policies. The World Development Report (1995) argued implicitly that the reasons for the growth of the informal sector in developing countries was labour market distortions, such as trade unions and government policies leading to inflexible labour markets. However, this has been contested on the ground that the informal sector existed before the growth of trade unions and the reason for the growth of the informal sector is capital market distortions. Since capital labour ratios are generally higher in the formal sector, labour productivity is higher and so are earnings in this sector. The chain of causation runs from differential capital intensity to productivity differences to wage differences. The reasons for the growth of the informal sector are important from the point of view of developing policies. Whatever the reason, the growth of the informal sector in the emerging labour market is inevitable. Women's employment in the informal sector is also likely to rise due to various reasons. With the adoption of the structural adjustment programme women tend to loose ground in the formal sectors of the economy. The growth of ancillarisation and industrial employment through sub-contracting appears to be gaining importance. Stagnating and falling incomes of households due to poor performance of the economy also leads to increased entry of women into the labour market. The process of globalization, export-oriented industrialization and relocation of industries from the developed to the developing countries also lead to the increase in the employment in the informal sector. Women's employment is often favoured in many of these industries. These factors lead to the increasing informalisation of the labour force. This informalisation takes place broadly in two ways. Work is pushed out of the enterprises and formal work situations into tiny workshops, the homes and informal situations i.e., there is an global trend in sub-contracting of work and a consequent increase in informal work, often in home working. Secondly, the workers who remain in the factories or in formal work situations are governed by looser contracts and obtain fewer social security benefits. That is, there is an attempt on the part of the employer to reduce his liabilities. The definition of the informal sector cited by ILO was descriptive. It specified a set of characteristics to distinguish informal enterprises such as small scale of operation, family ownership, reliance on indigenous resources, labour intensive and adaptive technology, skills acquired outside the formal system and operation in unregulated and competitive markets. The problem with applying such multiple criteria is that all of them could be found in units pursuing different objectives. It is also difficult to apply. In practice, most of the early ILO studies ended up using a single index of the employment size. On account of the complexity and looseness of the concept, the labour statisticians decided to distinguish one single statistical definition for the purpose of data collection from the several definitions that may vary according to the needs of the users and could be differentiated at the tabulation stage. The SNA (1993) characterizes the informal sector as consisting of units engaged in the production of goods or services with the primary objective of generating employment and incomes to the persons concerned. They form part of the household sector as unincorporated enterprises owned by households. They are distinguished from corporations and quasi-corporations on the basis of their legal status and the type of accounts they hold. These household enterprises do not have a legal status independently of the households or household members owning them. An operational definition of the informal sector that is irrespective of the kind of workplace, the extent of fixed assets, the duration of the activity of the enterprises and its operation as a main or secondary activity. Within the household sector, the informal sector comprises of informal own-account enterprises that are single member or partnership household units that do not hire workers on a continuous basis; enterprises of informal employers are household units owned and operated by employers, singly or in partnership, which employ one or more employees on a more or less continuous basis. For operational purposes the latter may be defined in terms of either, the size of unit below a specified level of employment or, non-registration of the enterprise or its employees. The SNA definition of the informal sector is based on the legal status of the enterprise. To distinguish employment in the informal sector one will have to assume that all persons working in such units are workers in this sector namely, informal employers and employees in the enterprises of informal employers, own account workers and unpaid family helps in informal enterprises. This definition of the informal sector, focusing on the enterprise, does not give us any clue about the status and working conditions of the workers in them. It will not be correct to assume that all workers in the formal sector are better off than all workers in the informal sector, or that all workers in the informal sector are equally badly off. In recent years many writings have expressed the view that such a dichotomized classification of the formal and informal sector is unrealistic and tends to hide more than it reveals. It also fails to capture three things, which are important from the point of view of social protection for workers, particularly women–the continuing process of informalisation of the formal economy; the great diversity within the informal economy itself; and the linkages between the formal and informal parts of the economy. The term informal sector is giving way to the term informal economy. Sethuraman (1998) argued that it is now widely accepted that such a dichotomy into the formal and informal is but a caricature of the real economy because both the formal and informal parts exhibit considerable diversity. Employment in the informal economy is not only inferior to that in the formal economy in terms of wages and benefits received, but also varies in terms of quality. Some jobs tend to be more informal than others in the sense that the extent of deviation from the established quality norms is greater. The dichotomous definition of the formal and informal sector actually distinguishes the status of the enterprise. This is useful for national accounts and in estimating the gross value added accruing from the two sectors. The concept of the informal economy in fact tries to characterise the workers depending on the degree of informality of their work status. This is more useful to persons concerned with wages, working conditions and access to social protection to workers. A second problem with the enterprise based definition is when it is used in an establishment survey to distinguish the unit. This definition tends to leave out more invisible groups of own-account enterprises such as those operating on the streets or in their homes. A labour force survey with clear questions on the place of work and nature of contract may be better able to net in all such workers. It is argued that the enterprise-based dichotomous definition is important from the point of view of estimating the contribution of this sector in the gross national product. However, an additional worker based approach is required to identify the status of workers within the two sectors and invisible groups of workers often missed out through an enterprise approach (Unni 2001).

Thus, the informal sector is its identification with pre-capitalist mode of production, own account of workers and no access to the benefits of social security and is characterised by low capital intensity, low level of productivity, a tiny and usually poor clientele, a low level of formal schooling, intermediate technology, preponderance of family labour and ownership, ease of entrance and last but not least, lack of support and recognition from the government.

BASIC CHARACTERISTICS

The rapid rise in research focusing on the urban informal sector in developing countries have led to a greater vagueness and inconsistency of definition of the term informal sector. Obviously, the major reason behind this state of affairs is the lack of a 'clear empirical basis' for the concept (Mehta 1985:327). However, several scholars have attempted to make generalization of the salient characteristics of group of activities and workers in the informal sector. The identification of characteristics of the informal sector has mostly been derived from the various empirical studies conducted in developing countries. The following are the basic characteristics of informal sector in studies on the subject:

(a) *Ease of Entry:* The informal sector is characterized by its fluidity and mobility of its labour. It is the entry point to the city for immigrants who left their native villages in the aspiration of urban income higher than their poor agricultural income. New entrants depend on their friends and relatives already settled down in the city to support them financially and search for job opportunities (Romatet 1983: 2115).

(b) *Autonomy and Flexibility:* Many informal sector participants in developed countries choose to participate in the informal sector because they find more autonomy, flexibility and freedom in this sector than in the formal sector. In other words, participants have the freedom of operation they can use and developed their creativity (Gerxhani 1999).

(c) *Small Scale of Operations:* Informal sector generally comprises with tiny establishments. The sector may be single worker establishments and those with only self-employed and own account workers form (Bienefeld 1974; Breman 1976:1873; Hart 1973: 66). Small scale of operation is considered a necessary condition for inclusion of an enterprise in the informal sector, because 'smallness' is usually accompanied by several other attributes, which make such enterprises disadvantaged (Sethuraman 1976:76). The small size indicates a relatively small size of employment with low capital intensity and low rate of return on capital employed.

(d) *Family Ownership of Enterprise:* In informal sector, functional division of labour and specialization is limited and most of the managerial and administrative functions are to be performed by the owner. The family labour is extensively used in the sector. These all features are not necessarily found to go together. Small size itself makes it possible to run an enterprise without a structural division of labour and management hierarchy. The organizations with wider ownership and using hired labour may disclose these features if their scale of operation is small. On the contrary, large even family owned organizations cannot be run on the basis of informal and un-structural organization and undefined functional division of labour. Thus, structure of organization is mainly a function of size and is not necessarily related to the pattern of ownership (Papola 1981).

(e) *Labour Intensive and Adaptive Technology:* The informal sector units use labour intensive, predominantly manual, low productivity techniques of production. According to John Week (1975:2), informal sector is characterized by small-scale operations labour intensive techniques, low levels of income and indigenous ownership. Informal sector may not adopt capital-intensive modern technology, either because it does not have access to it or because it does not suit the sector in the given relative cost position of capital and labour is hired at a much lower wage rate than the formal sector.

(f) *Lack of Support and Recognition from the Government:* Informal sector activities have grown without any government support. The organized capital market, bank finance, foreign technology, imported raw materials, protection from foreign competition etc. are not available to the informal sector enterprises on account of meagre material resources. Sometimes the informal sector units are found to engage in certain activities requiring legal permission without obtaining it or to acquire certain inputs requiring license from the illegal market, as a consequence of official limitation of access to the formal sector (Week 1975:3). The government's attempts to enforce certain regulations are naturally considered by these enterprises as 'hostile' conditions making their operations difficult (Sethuraman 1977: 198).

(g) *Competitive and Unregulated Product Market:* The informal sector in developing countries is generally found to have competitive and unregulated market. It is not always true that the informal sector produces goods and renders services of general use, while the formal sector enterprises predominantly cater to the demand of high income group of population and foreign market nor do all informal sector enterprises operate in a competitive market and all formal sector enterprises in a oligopolistic and protected market (Joshi and Joshi 1976; Weeks 1975:3).

(h) *Unprotected Labour Market:* The labour market in the informal sector is supposed to be unregulated and highly competitive because of absolute freedom to entry in the sector. The supply of labour in the informal sector consists of mostly new entrants in the labour market in-migrants or young persons entering the labour force. Since the opportunities for getting a job in the formal sector become restricted, they move towards a small establishment in the informal sector. As a result situation of underemployment and depressed wages prevail in the informal sector (Mazumdar 1977).

(i) *Unreported Income or Tax Evasion:* The informal sector is described as the sum of all taxable money income left unreported with the intension to evade taxes (Feige 1990). There is no record of monetary transaction, therefore the income is not reported for taxation. The subject becomes more complex while market activity is categoried into taxable and non-taxable activity. A classification system for viewing this distinction is presented in Table1.1 (McCrohan *et al.* 1991).

Table 1.1
Relationship between Taxable and Measured Market Income

	Taxable	*Not taxable*
Measured	Legal source market income: Informal economy Example: Payment to contractor, bartering of vehicle repairs for services	Legal source market income: Informal economy Example: Lawn cutting done by a teenager
Not Measured	Illegal source market income: Illegal sector of informal economy Example: Sale of drugs, sale of stolen automobiles	Intra-sector transfer Example: garage sale, sale of used refrigerator to a neighbour

Source: McCrohan *et al.* [1991].

(*j*) *Legal or Illegal:* Within the framework of informal sector activities may be legal or illegal. Economic activities may be classified by the manner in which goods and services are produced or exchanged. Income generated by economic activity may be segregated by the legality of the production or provision of goods and services and the legal status of goods and services themselves.

On the whole, these characteristics of informal sector may be grouped into three broad categories as follows (Mehta 1985:328):

- Those related to the characteristics of the enterprise, like size, family ownership, source of inputs, labour intensive technology etc. In this category, the emphasis is on the context within which people work, the stress being placed on the mode of production.
- Those related to the nature of exchange relationship with the State and the rest of urban economy like unregulated and competitive markets, lack of support and recognition from the

government, lack of structural organization, unregistered nature of enterprises etc.

- Those based on the employment situation or labour market processes like ease of entry, self-employed or casual nature of work, lack of formal contractual arrangement for employment etc.

CAUSES AND MOTIVES

The causes for participation in the informal sector can be economic and non-economic. Economic reasons are related to unemployment and an inflexible formal labour market, a declining real price of capital and the high cost of formal production. Besides, non-economic causes are concerned with a greater flexibility and satisfaction in work, a complete use of workers professional qualifications and increased leisure time (Gerxhani 1999). There are two groups of factors, which determine the decision to become active in the informal sector, more specifically, the structural as well as opportunity factors. The structural factors consist of economic pressure, socio-psychological pressure and institutional constraints. The opportunity factors consist of individual background, skills, education, living condition or non-individual components, environment, values, standards etc. The fundamental reasons to participation in the informal economy may be cited as:

- As a consequence of stagnation, unemployment and depreciation of capital stimulate participation in the informal activities. Thus, economic recession is the foremost cause of informalisation.
- The tax evasion is another cause to participation in the informal economy that has recently gained much more attention amongst the economists.
- Governmental excessive regulation of the market sector through the various legislations related to

labour conditions, quality regulation and production limits tend to a larger informal sector. This type of over regulation enhances the transaction costs of the participants in the formal economy, so that it becomes relatively more appealing to shift to the informal economy.

The main causes of informal labour may be divided in three main groups such as economic, institutional and social. This classification can be instrumental for the adoption of policy measures addressing the issue of informal labour. The main economic reasons of informal labour are the following:

- Lack of legal jobs.
- Lack or insufficient level of legal income.
- Higher remuneration if the job is done without registration.
- Strong and unfair competition, which may prompt firms to look for cost reduction, including through informal labour.

Economic transition has brought new phenomena such as unemployment, poverty and large income disparities. This has been instrumental for many people to accept jobs in the informal sector. Fast changes in income distribution may create incentives for the losers to accept additional informal jobs. Strong competition from firms, which benefit from the informal economy, including from black labour, may create pressure for other firms to do the same (a mimic effect). The institutional environment, in which firms, workers and households operate, is usually considered as a major cause of informal labour. This environment includes:

- High taxation on labour.
- High unemployment benefits.
- Complicated procedures for getting unemployment benefits (how easy it is to get benefits, their time-

span, methods of skill assessment, rules of registration of temporary job contracts by retired and unemployed people, etc.).

- Other specific labour markets regulations, such as rules of hiring and firing employees, including temporary and seasonal workers.
- Size and capacity of the tax administration.

High income taxes create large disparities between legal and informal wages and incentives to go informal. Empirical studies suggest that labour supply (the number of hours worked) is strongly correlated with the pay rates in both legal and informal labour markets. This means that a reduction of the divergence between the pay rates for legal and illegal work will lead to a decline of the volume of informal work. Low unemployment benefits create incentives for taking informal jobs. In addition, relatively high unemployment benefits do not motivate towards searching for jobs (this is the poverty trap). Barriers to registration of temporary labour contracts by employers may lead to increase of informal labour. Inflexible labour regulations also provide incentives to go informal. High firing costs, such as obligatory severance pay, do not encourage employers to hire workers legally. This is certainly obvious for small firms. Transformation has also brought new challenges for the administration in general, but both fiscal and labour administration can be instrumental for controlling the size of informal sector, although it takes a long time to build their capabilities. The third group of causes of informal activities consists of psychological and cultural motivations to go informal:

- Social tax morality (i.e., the acceptance of black labour and tax evasion by society).
- Risk-adverse or risk-taking attitudes in society.
- Willingness to work on a permanent labour contract.

In developing countries most of the people engage in the informal economy. They do so for a variety of reasons. For some it is an economic inevitability, their only resort or a better alternative to other low-wage formal employment available. Others are involved in informal work for personal fulfillment, social obligation or as a means of supplementing their primary income. The majority of informal economy participants are employees, working for others, in sweatshops or out of their homes in contract relationships to producers. But, many are also self-employed. The very nature of being a micro or very tiny activity lends itself to operating in the informal economy. These enterprises are largely invisible or operate at low levels of visibility. They may or may not have licenses, and are often engaged in casual hiring, non-reporting of income and other informal labour practices. They can be easily moved, opened or closed and thus, can hide from regulation. Finally, it is important to note that the formal and informal economies are connected. Participants may combine earnings from informal self-employment with wages from formal employment or transfer payments, such as public benefits or investment income or savings or, they may be employed both formally and informally at the same time. They engage in these activities to generate extra income in low-wage markets and to create an economic buffer to cover periods of unemployment. Informal work arrangements may also be a strategy imposed from the outside as big enterprises restructure and outsource functions to subcontractors both to minimize costs and maximize flexibility. Under these arrangements, they push workers out of the formal economy into the informal economy where they suffer without protections of the legal system. Workers are found who move fluidly back and forth between the two economies, some by necessity, and others by choice. While the factors above influence the size of the activity, entrepreneurs cite additional reasons for keeping the segment informal:

- Perhaps most importantly is the attitude of the individual toward the activity itself. Looked at as something that matches within other economic activities that they do, it is seen less as an enterprise than as just another way one works to make a little money. As one more patch in a complex of economic endeavors, it is not perceived as something that needs to be any more structured than the work itself requires and if it demanded more rigors in paperwork and other requirements, it would lose its value to the entrepreneur and his/her family.
- Often the activity is so small-scale (or occasional or erratic) that it is not worth reporting as far as the entrepreneur is concerned.
- There is a tradition of exchange and while these exchanges may be calculated in rough terms to ensure that the trades are even rarely are records kept of these valuations. Rather the exchanges represent important inputs into households that can operate quite invisibly to the outside world and are attractive for that reason.
- Finally, in a few cases, the activity is new and being tested to overview if it is worth converting into a larger or more formal operation. The entrepreneur will increasingly move to following more of the rules of the game as the potential of the business becomes clearer.

TYPOLOGY

All informal activity has one common feature namely the entrepreneurs who works in the informal economy perceive the benefits of doing so to offset the costs of going formal. Recent studies have identified a number of reasons why some entrepreneurial activity may take place in the shadows. The most important determinants are the prevalence of burdensome and costly government regulations and the level and administrative complexity of taxation. Informality comes at a cost, the inability to use government and some private sector services available to firms that fully comply with regulations. In countries entrepreneurs may well opt to be formal, even if regulations are many and taxes are high. In contrast, entrepreneurs in countries where the quality of public services to enterprises is poor have a much easier choice. In the absence of discernible benefits of going formal, they prefer to save their time and money and stay informal. Many transition economies have experienced surging share of entrepreneurial activity in the informal sector. Some of this activity is illegal. Such activity will not become formal, regardless of improvements in the enterprises climate. Other activities, like small production units operate merely for the subsistence of their owners and do not generate enough revenue to make their inclusion in the tax base meaningful. However, there exists a considerable share of entrepreneurial activity that is semi-formal e.g., the organization is registered but most changes. Informal activities usually fall into three broad categories namely employees are not, and can become formal with appropriate policy underground enterprises, subsistence enterprises and unofficial enterprises.

Subsistence enterprises result from coping strategies adopted by families to compensate for low wages or external shocks e.g., unemployment etc. Unofficial enterprises generally result from the desire to escape or avoid the administrative and/or financial burden of regulation e.g., license and permit regimes, taxes, labour regulations etc. Firms around the world lie on a spectrum of entrepreneurial activity, ranging from informal to formal. A typology of the informal sector is presented in Table 1.2. Another typology represents categories of informal work based on the context of the work. Informal work may involve a person working for someone else or a person being self-employed and within each of the categories there are two arrangements (Table 1.3).

Table 1.2
A Taxonomy of Typology of Informal Sector

	Informal sector	
	Subsistence enterprises	*Unofficial enterprises*
Degree	100 per cent of informality	High proportion of sales and workers not registered
Type of activity	Single street traders, cottage/micro enterprises, subsistence farmers	Small manufacturers, service providers, distributors, contractors
Technology	Labour intensive	Mostly labour intensive
Owner profile	Poor, low education, low level of skills	Poor and non-poor, well educated, high level of skills
Markets	Low barrier to entry, highly competitive, high product homogeneity	Low barrier to entry, highly competitive, some product differentiation
Finance needs	Working capital	Working capital, some investment capital, supplier creditPersonal
Other needs	Personal insurance, social protection	perhaps business insurance

Source: Djankov *et al.* [2003].

Table 1.3
Structure of Informal Work Typology

	Primary work for firm	*Extra work for current employer*
Person works for someone else	Works off the books Works under the table Paid in cash and not taxed	Works extra hours on weekends or evening (paid in cash and not taxed)
	Person operate own tiny business	Does sporadic odd jobs, services or products
Person self employed	Cash only exchange Ongoing, regular Business is seen primary incomeMay invest income into business	Works extra hours on weekends or evening (paid in cash and not taxed)

Source: ILO [2002].

CLASSIFICATION OF PARTICIPANTS

Following the worker approach workers in the informal economy can be broadly distinguished into wage employment and non-wage employment, each consisting of the components of own account workers, employers/ owners of informal enterprises with at least one hired worker; unpaid family helpers in both types of informal enterprises, employees in the enterprises of informal employers, outworkers or home workers (persons working at home, or on premises of his choice other than the employer's, to produce goods or services on a contract or order for a specific employer or contractor), independent wage workers not attached to only one employer and providing services to individuals, households and enterprises, e.g., maid servants and watchmen working for households and informal employment in formal sector enterprises (workers whose pay and benefits do not conform to existing labour regulations). This categorization is similar to that developed by Sethuraman (1998). In the literature the first four categories are generally taken to represent employment in the informal sector. The need to distinguish the category of independent wageworkers can be debated. In many Latin American countries domestic helps are distinguished in the national surveys and together with independent wageworkers are added to the informal sector (Sethuraman 1998). The first process of informalisation of the labour force, pushing work out of formal work situations, leads to an increase in the first component, non-wage employment. It can also lead to increase in the first two varieties of the second component i.e., informal wage employment. The second process of informalisation, resulting in looser contracts and fewer benefits, leads to an increase in the last category of workers, informal employment within the formal enterprises as defined by the enterprise-based approach. Obviously it is not easy to obtain empirical estimates of these categories of workers from the national official labour statistics. However, an approximation of the first component of the informal economy can be arrived at, non-wage employment or self-employment, by the addition of employers, own account workers and unpaid family helpers in the activity status classification of the national labour force survey. While it may be relatively safe to assume that own account workers and unpaid family helpers are part of the informal economy, this assumption may not be very accurate for the category of employer. Employers, however, form a very small proportion of the workforce. The second component of the informal economy is even more difficult to demarcate from the official data since there is really a continuum in the degree of informality in the employer-employee relationships. The official data distinguish only employees. The Indian labour force surveys further classifies them into casual and regular. All regular workers do not necessarily belong to the formal economy, as they often do not receive a variety of benefits due to the formal worker such as provident funds, paid leave etc. An approximation of the second component of the informal economy can be made by assuming that all casual employees definitely constitute a part of the informal economy since they are least likely to obtain any of the benefits accruing to formal economy workers. Another indicator or measure of the nature of informality of the work status or sector is the earnings differentials. The informal economy can be distinguished by the inferior quality of work and inferior terms of employment, both remuneration and benefits. Among the non-wage component inferior technologies lead to low productivity and hence to low earnings or incomes.

Since informal sector is very diverse and it covers many types of work, so it is difficult to classify it into a specific group as uniform. However, the workers in the informal sector may be classified broadly into four categories as under:

Home Based Workers

The workers in this category carry out their activities using their traditional skill and labour. The majority of the home based workers work in the privacy of their homes and they are invisible. This category of workers engages in earthen pots making, rural artisans etc.

Self Employed or Own Account Workers

Self-employed or own account workers are those who do not have any permanent place for carrying out their activities. Some of them have to change their place of activity almost on a daily basis. In this category of workers includes street vendors, hawkers, rag pickers, rickshaw pullers, sex workers etc.

Piece Wage Workers

There has been a tremendous growth of private informal manufacturing such as garment making, knitting etc. These categories of workers are employed by entrepreneurs. They are usually employed on a piece rate basis. This type of workers carry out their work independently, but employers exercise control over them by supplying raw material and sometimes advancing a minimum cash. This kind of labour is often found in beedi making, carpet and mat weaving, lace industry etc.

Time Wage Workers

This type of workers sells their labour power in exchange of a low paid time rate of wage. The most of the workers in this category are quasi permanent. These workers are placed in a most disadvantageous position. Their activities rely heavily on manual labour. This category includes gardeners, cleaners, sweepers, construction labourers, bricks workers, agricultural labourers, domestic servants etc.

PAID-UNPAID ECONOMY

In economy two types of work exist namely, paid work and unpaid work. While a worker is engaged for performing chore on the basis of an agreed wage payment, the activities carried out by the concerned worker may be termed as paid work. On the other hand, the time spent by a worker in several activities in domestic sector may be termed as unpaid care work. In economy unpaid work is often informal while paid work may be formal or informal. The connections between the unpaid care economy and the paid economy (Himmelweit 2002) are represented in Figure 1.1, which shows the flows of the characteristic net contribution of each sector to the rest of the economy. The unpaid economy consists of the domestic sector that contributes to individual socialization and to the production and maintenance of human capabilities. The paid economy contains both the social and economic infrastructure and producing sector. However, each sector may and does make other outputs.

Gender impact analysis must examine the effects of any economic policy on both the paid and unpaid economies, disaggregating these effects by gender. The most significant gender division of labour is that between the two economies. Women still devote the majority of their working time to the unpaid economy and men devote theirs to the paid economy in both developed and developing countries (United Nations Development Programme 1995). Given this disparity, the overall distributional effect of policies that improve the conditions of paid work over unpaid work will be to worsen gender inequality, unless those policies are specifically targeted on improving women's situation. Thus there are two aspects to the gender division of labour between paid and unpaid economies. It is not only that woman overall tend to do more unpaid caring work than men. It is also that an inside division of labour within households allocates that work and if a woman shares her household with another member, it is likely that that other member does less unpaid caring work than she does. This is not of course exact for women who share their household with other women, although the allocation of caring work may in practice still be unequal. A woman or anyone doing the bulk of caring work can lose bargaining power because her contribution of unpaid labour is less visible than her counterpart's economic contribution.

A United Nations (1991) report on women's work patterns based on surveys made across countries of the world gives a summary of women's devotion of time to both paid and unpaid economic activity. The findings are as follows:

- Women spend more of their time working than men folk in all developed and developing regions except northern America and Australia where the working hours are almost equal.
- In developing countries women spend more time in the labour force than their household work. Men by contrast are spending less amount of time working in the labour force than before in all developed regions and slightly rising amounts of time in household in northern America and Western Europe.
- In Africa, Asia and the Pacific women as on average 12-13 hours more than men per week.
- Men in developing regions generally do more household chores than men in the developed regions.
- Women everywhere in the world have nearly total responsibility for housework. While men help out women keep the responsibility of housework.

Fig. 1.1: The Interdependence of the Paid and Unpaid Economies

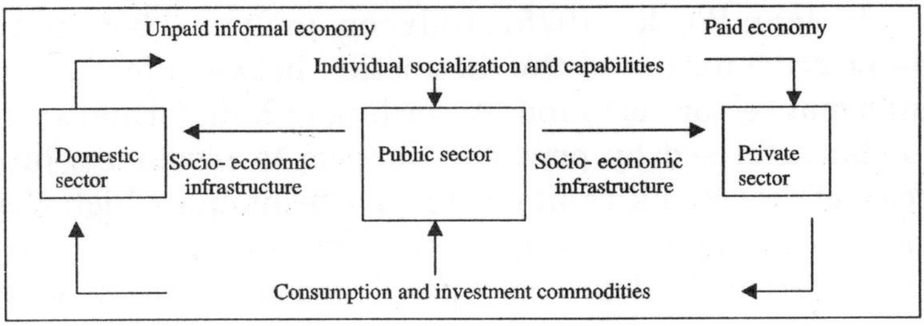

Source: Himmelweit [2002].

FORMAL-INFORMAL DICHOTOMY

Contrasting Characteristics

The most commonly used classification is the one, which segregates the economy into formal and informal sectors. As a classification of economic activities, one would intuitively assume that distinction refers to the fact of formal or informal character of producers. However, it has not meant so, the distinction has been made on the basis of certain empirical facts of size, nature of market and relation with the State (Papola 1981). Various empirical studies highlight distinguishing characteristics of formal and informal sectors.

Joshi and Joshi (1976) have laid down the distinguishing characteristics of the two sectors. According to them, informal sector contains large manufacturing firms operating in oligopolistic markets sheltered from foreign competition by high tariffs and quantitative restrictions, selling their product mainly to middle and upper income groups. On the other hand, informal sector contains a very large number of small producers operating on narrow margins in highly competitive product markets, selling a variety of goods and services mainly to low-income groups. They also added that while formal sector uses capital intensive, imported technology, the informal sector adopts labour intensive indigenous technology.

In John Weeks (1975) study, on analytical base to the descriptive nature of the distinction between formal and informal sectors is found. According to him, formal sector is characterised by privileged access to resources, large scale of operations, capital-intensive techniques, high wage rates and salary packages. Besides, informal sector is characterised by deprived of privileged access to resources, tiny scale of operations, labour intensive techniques, low level of earnings and indigenous ownership.

Table1.4
Distinguishing Characteristics of Formal and Informal Sectors

Formal sector	*Informal sector*
(a) Difficult to entry	(a) Ease of entry
(b) Legal form of enterprises, corporate ownership	(b) Cottage enterprises, family ownership
(c) Large size of operations	(c) Small size of operations
(d) Capital intensive and foreign technology	(d) Labour intensive and indigenous technology
(e) Regulated and restricted competition	(e) Unregulated and high competitive product market
(f) High level of earnings	(f) Low level of earnings
(g) Formally acquired skill	(g) Skill acquired through on the job training
(h) Less chance of exploitation of labour for existence of trade union	(h) More chance of exploitation of labour for non-existence of trade union
(i) Access to government favours	(i) Development of activities without government support
(j) Definite structure	(j) Structure less
(k) Permanent and stable	(k) Temporary and instable
(l) Official channels of communication	(l) Own communication, commonly known as grapevine

Mazumdar (1977) has explained the distinction sharply focusing on the fact that entry into the informal sector labour market is unrestricted, while that in the formal sector labour market is restricted by artificially raised hiring standards, norms and producers.

Thus, the distinguishing characteristics of the two sectors may be summarized from the various studies as shown in Table 1.4.

Linkages

Apart from the contrasting characteristics of formal informal sector, it is worthwhile to identify the nature of linkages between the two sectors or among the various economic activities in the urban economy. The linkages may initially be classified as direct and indirect. The direct linkages may be in terms of resource inputs from formal to informal sectors or technology and market linkages (Bose 1978). On the other hand, indirect linkages refer to the demand of goods and services generated in the informal sector by a clientele whose income is dependent on the formal sector.

Many of the research studies have identified the nature of direct relationships between formal and informal sectors. Bienefeld's (1975) study in Tanzania with a tentative framework assumes that many small scale operators are engaged in a process of production and of technological development but their ability to develop cumulatively over the terms of trade, by their dependence on large scale industry for inputs (often illegally obtained) and by the fact that when the markets they serve grow beyond a certain size this will not be a gradual but accelerating stimulus to further will not be a gradual development of the forces of production. Instead it will trigger a discontinuous shift to international technology, which will incorporate this market by virtue of its efficiency and / or its market power the latter based on effectively unlimited access to capital and on the establishment of brand name products through heavy advertising (Bienefeld 1975:56). Thus, exploitative character of linkages has been identified by Bienefeld.

Bose (1978) in his study explains the exploitative character of linkages in the urban economy of Calcutta. According to him, the informal sector enterprises perform two basic functions. First, they produce cheap goods for rural and urban poor, who are finding it increasingly difficult to purchase high cost, standard industrial goods. This is based on the low wages in this sector. The second function is to supply the large units with huge trading profit through an unequal exchange relationship. Thus, the poor in the informal sector operate in a separate market both for resource inputs and outputs, which is highly unfavourable to them, the gains being appropriated by the large sector.

Other studies including Bose's shows that official programmes which aim at stimulating industry in the informal sector are of little use in practice.

Breman (1976: 1874) explains that neither can increase aid by the State be expected as long as the political system is dominated by interests, which are linked to the formal sector.

Papola (1979) identifies the informal manufacturing activities, which are linked up vertically to the formal sector through market and technology linkages. He concludes that although the informal sector provides a significant part of goods and services in the urban economy and generates employment to practically the entire residual labour force, its growth largely depends on the fortunes of the formal sector.

Jagannathan (1987) focuses on the direct linkage between formal and informal sectors in developing countries are the result of the existence of a large parallel urban informal sector.

In Datta Choudhury's (1989) formulation, formal and informal sectors are linked together because capital costs and wages differ between them. Informal sector will exist as long as these differences exit. If cheap credit is provided to informal sector, it will in due course of time specialize in producing intermediate products. It may even completely take over their production from formal sector.

Peattie (1980) in her study of small manufacturing enterprises in Bogota, Colombia finds that these enterprises served two distinct types of clientele. Firstly, enterprises were producing on inferior and cheaper product in a way, which makes it accessible to persons who can neither buy in large quantities nor transport for long distances. The other type served a small and individualized market (as in custom made furniture and shoes) or where a great deal of flexibility in marketing is advantageous (as in street vending and illegal occupations).

Operations Research Group (1980) in their study of informal sector in Madras looks at the backward and forward linkages for informal enterprises in manufacturing, trading and service activities. They find that it was more in terms of resource inputs that a variety of linkages with large dealers were common. However, the activities on the whole were more individual customer oriented. Only the craft based items, there were some links with other dealers.

Stark (1982) has extended Harris-Todaro model by incorporating a linkage coefficient to denote the connection between formal and informal sectors. The coefficient can assume both positive and negative values. Thus, expansion of formal sector can lead to both expansion and construction of informal sector. One more possibility is considered, viz., if rural migrants take up informal sector jobs, a negative signal about their human capital acquisition is flashed and their future employment and earning prospects are harmed. Therefore, the journey from formal sector to informal sector is easy but not vice versa. The model disposes that the dominance of formal sector cannot be presumed in migration decisions. It arrives at the result that the determinants of informal sector growth originate in formal sector but the role of informal sector in urban growth cannot be predetermined analytically.

So far as the indirect linkages are concerned, it refers to those generated by the goods and services produced in the informal sector for a clientele whose income is dependent on the formal sector. The activities namely building and furnishing of middle class houses, repairs and maintenance services, trading of fresh vegetables, fish, fruits etc. and of course are dependent on the income of a clientele who in turn is dependent on formal sector activities. Thus, a growth in the formal sector productivity and wages obviously creates the additional demand for these activities.

Besides, these types of direct indirect relationships, there also exist social dependency linkages, which have their basis in the lack of economic security. A complete lack of public welfare or unemployment compensation, coupled with a highly irregular and insecure nature of income, forces these people into either social dependency relationships or petty entrepreneurships (Mehta 1985: 329).

Therefore, it can be concluded that the informal sector is in no way an independent and exclusive entity rather it is linked to the formal sector and the rest of the economy. The possibility of growth and expansion of the sector largely depends on the nature and type of linkages that are prevailing in reality.

INFORMAL VS. HOUSEHOLD AND UNDERGROUND ECONOMY

While the divergence between informal and underground activities is the subtlest, it is also imperative to discriminate between other forms of non-measured, non-taxed, and/or non-regulated activities. Several scholars have argued that a distinction can be made between households, informal, underground and illegal activities (ILO 1993b; Thomas 1992). In fact, as much of the research in developing countries has revealed there is a continuum, not only between informal and formal activities, but also between household, informal, underground and illegal activities. However, for policy, measurement and analytical purposes it is important to distinguish between them. Initiating with the household sector, the informal sector could be defined as the set of activities, enterprises, income or persons, which satisfy certain characteristics and which are by definition, not part of the household sector, and so on.

The term hidden economy refers to the output from all productive activities, enterprises, income or people, which are unmeasured in gross domestic product and/or untaxed and/or unregulated. Thus the hidden economy comprises a wide range of productive activities from housework to organized crime. These can be grouped into four main categories namely, the household sector, the informal sector, the underground sector and the illegal sector.

Add to, the household sector as the set of household productive economic activities that produce goods and services for own consumption within the same household and which are unmeasured and/or untaxed and/or unregulated because they are outside the SNA production boundary. The household sector includes those activities that fall within the general production boundary but not within the SNA production boundary. Some scholars have argued for the inclusion of non-quantitatively significant household activities in the SNA, particularly in developing countries where they may contribute considerably to livelihoods . In developing and transition countries where social services are extremely limited and incomes are very low, household activities are an important source of income and employment for a significant share of the population.

The informal sector is defined as the set of productive economic activities, which fall within the SNA (1993) production boundary and are unmeasured untaxed and/or unregulated, not because of deliberate attempts to evade the payment of taxes or infringe labour or other legislation, but because they are undertaken to meet basic needs. The ILO (1993b) and SNA (1993) also argue for the need to distinguish informal sector activities from underground activities on the basis that the former are not necessarily performed with the deliberate intention of avoiding the payment of taxes, social security contributions or complying with certain legal standards, while the latter are. The ILO (1993b) defines the informal sector as the set of units engaged in the production of goods or services with the primary objective of generating employment and incomes to the persons concerned. Production units of the informal sector are defined as a subset of household unincorporated enterprises. Household enterprises are units engaged in the production of goods or services which are not constituted as separate legal entities independently of the households or household members that own them, and for which no complete set of accounts are available which would permit a clear distinction of the production activities of the enterprises from the other activities of their owners and the identification of any flows of income and capital between the enterprise and the owners. Indeed, since its conception the informal sector has been of interest in developing countries because it is an important source of income and employment for the poor. It is a survival strategy in countries where there is insufficient formal employment opportunities, where wages may be too low to cover the cost of living and where social safety nets such as unemployment or pension benefits are either lacking or also insufficient to cover the cost of living. As such, it should include all productive activities, which generate income and employment for the poor, and not just those that take place in household enterprises with certain characteristics.

The concepts of underground and illegal production as defined in the SNA (1993) consists of legal productive economic activities that are part of the production boundary and are unmeasured and/or untaxed and or unregulated because they are deliberately concealed from public authorities for the following kind of reasons to avoid the payment of income, value added or other taxes; to avoid the payment of social security contributions; to avoid having to meet certain legal standards such as minimum wages, maximum hours, safety or health standards, etc. to avoid complying with certain administrative procedures such as completing statistical questionnaires or other administrative forms.

The illegal sector consists of productive activities that generate goods and services forbidden by law or that are unlawful when carried out by unauthorised producers. There are two types of illegal activities: those that produce goods and services whose sale, distribution or possession is forbidden by law, and activities which are usually legal, but become illegal when carried out by unauthorized producers (SNA 1993). Furthermore illegal activities are included in the SNA production boundary if the transactions involved are based on mutual consent.

It is observed that the borderline among household, informal, underground and illegal sectors may not be very clear and activities may often belong to more than one sector. The Figure 1.2 illustrates how these sectors are interrelated (Bernabè 2002). It may not be obvious whether an activity is part of the household or informal sector (area A in figure 1.2). Subsistence farming, for instance, may be considered part of the household sector if it is not quantitatively significant in respect to total agricultural production (as may be the case in many developed countries), whereas it may be part of the informal sector if it is quantitatively significant (as may be the case in many developing and some transition countries). Similarly, it may be difficult to determine whether an activity is part of the illegal, household, or informal sectors (area B). The boundary is similarly difficult to define between informal and underground and between underground and illegal activities. Thus, construction activities undertaken by unregistered construction workers, for instance, may be considered informal or underground (area C), depending on whether or not they are deliberately concealed and whether they are undertaken to meet basic needs (they could of course be both). Finally, as highlighted in the SNA (1993), production that does not comply with certain safety, health or other standards, for instance, could be described as either underground or illegal (area D).

Fig. 1.2: Relationship among Informal, Household, Illegal and Underground Economy

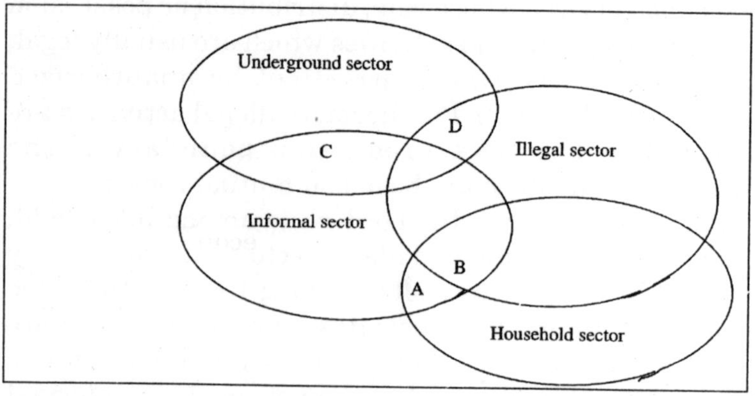

Source: Bernabè [2002].

SUMMARY

The term informal sector was first used by Keith Hart (1970) in a study of urban Ghana and it has been further refined by ILO (1972) while studying the employment situation in Kenya. The informal sector is characterized by ease of entry, small-scale operations, family ownership of enterprise, labour intensive and adaptive technology, lack of support and recognition from the government, competitive and unregulated product market, unprotected labour market, undisclosed income or tax evasion etc. In addition to these, the other characteristics include deplorable working condition and low level of wage, low capital accumulation and reinvestment, insecure and temporary nature of employment etc. Besides, the informal sector may be classified into four categories on the basis of their nature of works namely, home based workers, self-employment workers, piece wageworkers and time wageworkers. The causes of informalisation may be of economic recession, evasion of tax as well as excessive governmental regulation of market sector.

The urban economy can be classified broadly as formal and informal sectors. As far as the contrasting characteristics of the two sectors are concerned, the entry into the informal sector labour market is unrestricted and level of earning is also very low, while that in formal sector labour market, entry is restricted and level of earning is high. Apart from the distinguishing characteristics, there exist strong direct and indirect inter-linkages between formal and informal sectors.

The employment in the informal economy has risen rapidly in all regions of the developing countries and various forms of non-standard employment have emerged in most regions of the developed countries. In the developing economy, it was only the once rapidly growing economies that experienced substantial growth of modern sector employment. However, in the wake of the recent economic crisis, most of these countries experienced a substantial decline in formal wage employment and a concomitant rise in informal employment. How many retrenched workers have been reinstated in formal jobs as these economies have begun to recover from the crisis is not yet known. Why has the informal economy continued to expand and grow? There is no simple answer to this question as different causal factors are at work in different contexts. However, some mix of the following sets of factors would explain the persistence or expansion of the informal economy in most countries, regions, or industries. The first set of factors relates to the pattern of economic growth. Some countries have experienced little or no economic growth, while others have pursued capital-intensive growth or what some observers call jobless growth. In both such contexts, not enough jobs are created for all those seeking work. Many frustrated formal job seekers find employment or create their own work in the informal economy. Another pattern of economic growth namely high tech growth tends to create more high-skill service sector jobs than lower-skill manufacturing jobs. In such contexts, those without the skills to compete for high-tech formal jobs find work or continue to work in the informal economy. There is another, more optimistic, scenario namely, growth from below. In some countries the tiny business and micro-business sectors are more dynamic and create more jobs than the formal sector. The second set of factors has to do with economic restructuring and economic crisis. Available evidence suggests that during periods of economic adjustment whether due to economic reforms or economic crises, the informal economy tends to expand. This is because retrenched workers move into the informal economy when public enterprises are closed or the public sector is downsized. This is also because households need to supplement formal sector incomes with informal earnings in response to inflation or cutbacks in public services. The third set of factors relates to the globalization of the world economy. Global trade and investment patterns tend to privilege capital, especially companies that can move quickly and easily across borders and to disadvantage labour especially lower-skilled workers that cannot migrate easily or at all. To enhance their global competitiveness more and more investors are moving to countries that have low labour costs or shifting to informal employment arrangements. Furthermore, there has been a radical restructuring of production and distribution in many key industries characterized by outsourcing or subcontracting through global commodity chains. The net result is that more and more workers are being paid very low wages and many of them have to absorb the non-wage costs of production. Globalization also tends to privilege large companies who can capture new markets quickly and easily to the disadvantage of small and micro entrepreneurs who face difficulties gaining knowledge of much less access to emerging markets. In sum, globalization puts pressure on low-skilled workers and petty producers by weakening their bargaining power and subjecting them to increasing competition. Why should the persistence or expansion of the informal economy be of interest or concern? There is a link between working in the informal economy and being poor. Average incomes are lower in the informal economy than in the formal sector. As a result, a higher percentage of people working in the informal economy, relative to the formal sector, are poor. However, there is no simple relationship between working in the informal economy and being poor or working in the formal sector and escaping poverty (Sethuraman 1998 and Thomas 1995). The relationship between informal employment and poverty appears only when informal workers are classified by employment status and by industry or trade. Informal incomes worldwide tend to decline as one moves across the following types of employment: from employer to self-employed to informal and casual wageworkers to industrial outworker. The link between working in the informal economy and being poor is stronger for women than for men. A higher percentage of women than men worldwide work in the informal economy. Moreover, there is a gender gap in incomes and wages in the informal economy. This is because women worldwide are under-represented in higher income employment statuses in the informal economy (employer and self-employed) and over represented in the lower income statuses (casual wage worker and industrial outworker). Available evidence suggests that globalization of the economy tends to reinforce the links between poverty, informality and gender. This is because global competition tends to encourage formal firms to shift formal wageworkers to informal employment arrangements without minimum wages, assured work, or benefits and to encourage informal units to shift workers from semi-permanent contracts without minimum wages or benefits to piece-rate or casual work arrangements without either assured work, minimum wages, or benefits. This is also because globalization often leads to shifts from secure self-employment to more precarious self-employment, as producers and traders lose their market niche. With these shifts, and as more and more men enter the informal economy, women tend to be pushed to the lowest income end of the informal economy. But globalization can also lead to new opportunities for those who work in the informal economy in the form of new jobs for wageworkers or new markets for the self-employed. However, a collaborative effort on the part of grassroots organizations of those who work in the informal economy with sympathetic representatives of non-governmental, research, government, private sector and international development organizations is needed to enable the most vulnerable segments of society to seize these opportunities. There needs to be a much more detailed interpretation of who is in the informal economy and what they are doing, as well as a more comprehensive analysis of how globalization, particularly trade and investment policies, are affecting the employment arrangements and income sources of those who work in the informal economy.

REFERENCES

Banerjee, N. (1985), *Women Workers in the Unorganised Sector*. Sangam Books, Hyderabad.

Bernabè, S. (2002), *Informal Employment in Countries in Transition: a Conceptual Framework*. CASE Paper 56, Centre for Analysis of Social Exclusion, London School of Economics, London.

Bienefeld, M. (1975), The Informal Sector and Peripheral Capitalism: the Case of Tanzania. *Institute of Development Studies Bulletin*, 6: 53-73.

Bose, A.N. (1978), *Calcutta and Rural Bengal, Small Sector Symbioses*. Minerva Publications, Calcutta.

Breman, J. (1976), A Dualistic Labour System? A Critique of the Informal Sector, Concept I: the Informal Sector. *Economic and Political Weekly*, XI (48): 1870-1875.

Datta Choudhuri, T. (1989), A Theoretical Analysis of the Informal Sector. *World Development*, 17 (3): 351-355.

Djankov, S., Lieberman, I., Mukherjee, J. and Nenova, T. (2003), Going Informal: Benefits and Costs. In Boyan Belev (ed.). *The Informal Economy in the EU Accession Countries: Size, Scope, Trends and Challenges to the Process of EU Enlargement*. Center for the Study of Democracy, Sofia.

Eapen, M. (2001), Women in Informal Sector in Kerala: Need for Re-examination. *Economic and Political Weekly*, XXXVI (20): 2390-2392.

Feige, E.L. (1990), Defining and Estimating Underground and Informal Economies: the New Institutional Economic Approach. *World Development*, 18 (7): 989-1002.

Gerxhani, K. (1999), *The Informal Sector in Developed and Less Developed Countries*. Tinbergen Institute Discussion Paper No. 1999-083/2, Tinbergen Institute, The Netherlands.

Gibson, B. and Kelly, B. (1994), *A Classical Theory of the Informal Sector*. The Manchester School of Economic and Social Studies, LXII (1): 81-96.

Hart, K. (1970), Small-Scale Entrepreneurs in Ghana and Development Planning. *The Journal of Development Studies*, 6 (4): 104-120.

Hart, K. (1973), Informal Income Opportunities and Urban Employment in Ghana. *Journal of Modern African Studies*, 11 (1): 61-89.

Himmelweit, S. (2002), Making Visible the Hidden Economy: the Case for Gender Impact Analysis of Economic Policy. *Feminist Economics*, 8 (1): 49-70.

Hussmanns, R. (1998), *Developments in the Design and Implementation of Informal Sector and Similar Surveys: a Review of National Practices and Experiences*.DOC.ICLS/16/RD2, International Labour Office, Geneva.

International Labour Organization (1972), *Employment, Income and Equity: a Strategy for Increasing Productive Employment in Kenya*. Geneva.

International Labour Organization (1993a), *Highlights of the Conference and Text of the Three Resolutions Adopted*. Report of the XVth International Conference of Labour Statisticians, 19-28 January, Geneva.

International Labour Organization (1993b), *Resolution Concerning Statistics of Employment in the Informal Sector*. Geneva.

International Labour Organization (1999), *Employment in the Global Economy: How Training Matters*. World Employment Report, Geneva.

International Labour Organization (2002), *Women and Men in the Informal Economy: a Statistical Picture*. Employment Sector Paper, Geneva.

Jagannathan, N.V. (1987), *Informal Markets in Developing Countries*. Oxford University Press Inc., New York.

Joshi, H and Joshi, V. (1976), *Surplus Labour and City: A Study of Bombay*. Oxford University Press, New Delhi.

Mazumdar, D. (1975), *The Urban Informal Sector*. World Bank Staff Working Paper No. 211, World Bank, Washington D.C.

Mazumdar, D. (1977), Notes on the Urban Informal Sector. In Subbiah Kanappan (ed.). *Urban Labour Market Behaviour in Developing Countries*. International Institute of Labour Studies, Geneva.

McCrohan, K., Smith, J. and Adams, T. (1991), Consumer Purchases in Informal Markets: Estimates for the 1980s, Prospects for the 1990s. *Journal of Retailing*, 67(1): 22-50.

Mehta, M. (1985), Urban Informal Sector: Concepts, Indian Evidence and Policy Implications. *Economic and Political Weekly*, XX (8): 326- 332.

Nattrass, N.J. (1987), Street Trading in Transkei: A Struggle against Poverty, Persecution and Prosecution. *World Development*, 15 (7): 861-875.

Operations Research Group (1980) *Informal Sector Enterprises in Madras: A Profile and Strategy*. Mimeo, Madras.

Papola, T.S. (1979), *Informal Sector in an Urban Economy: A Study in Ahmedabad*. Giri Institute of Development Studies, Mimeo, Lucknow.

Papola, T.S. (1980), Informal Sector: Concept and Policy. *Economic and Political Weekly*, 15 (8): 817-823.

Papola, T.S. (1981), *Urban Informal Sector in a Developing Economy*. Vikash Publishing House, New Delhi.

Peattie, L.R. (1980), Anthropological Perspectives on the Concepts of Dualism, the Informal Sector and Marginality in Developing Urban Economies. *International Regional Science Review*, 5 (1): 1-31.

Psacharopoulos, G. and Tzannatos, Z. (1992), *Women's Employment and Pay in Latin America: Overview and Methodology*. World Bank Regional and Sectoral Studies, Washington D.C.

Rakowski, C.A. (1994), Convergence and Divergence in the Informal Sector Debate: A Focus on Latin America, 1984-92. *World Development*, 22 (4): 501-516.

Romatet, E. (1983), Calcutta's Informal Sector: Theory and Reality. *Economic and Political Weekly*, 18 (50): 2115-2128.

Sarkar, S. (2004a), Extending Social Security Coverage to the Informal Sector in India, *Social Change*, 34 (4): 122-130.

Sarkar, S. (2004b), Theorising in Informal Sector: Concept and Context, *Social Action*, 54 (4): 356-373.

Sethuraman, S.V. (1976), The Urban Informal Sector: Concept, Measurement and Policy. *International Labour Review*, 114: 69-81.

Sethuraman, S.V. (1998), *Gender, Informality and Poverty: a Global Review*. World Bank, Washington D.C.

Squire, L. (1981), *Employment Policy in Developing Countries: a Survey of Issues and Evidence*. Oxford University Press, New York.

Stark, O. (1982), On Modeling the Informal Sector. *World Development*, 10 (5): 413-416.

System of National Accounts (1993), *System of National Accounts*, 1993. World Bank, Washington, D.C.

Thomas, J. (1992), *Informal Economic Activity*. Harvester Wheatsheaf, Hemel Hempstead.

Thomas, J.J. (1995), *Surviving in the City: The Urban Informal Sector in Latin America*. CT: Pluto Press, East Haven.

Tokman, V.E. (1978), An Exploration into the Nature of Informal-Formal Relationships. *World Development*, 6 (9-10): 1065-1075.

United Nations (1991) *The World's Women 1970-1990*. New York.

United Nations Development Programme (1995), *Human Development Report 1995*. Oxford University Press, Oxford.

Unni, J. (2001), Gender and Informality in the Labour Market in South Asia. *Economic and Political Weekly*, 36 (26): 2360-2377.

Weeks, J. (1975), Policies for Expanding Employment in the Informal Urban Sector of Developing Economics. *International Labour Review*, 3 (1): 1-13.

World Development Report (1995), *Workers in an Integrating World*. World Bank, Washington D.C.

Chapter - 2

Women as Domestic Help

INTRODUCTION

Starting from complete neglect, then phenomenon of informal economic activity has grown to be a subject of study by many researchers, both governmental and non-governmental (Sarkar 2004: 359). There has been rapid growth in the number of women employed in India with majority of them engaged in the informal sector of the economy where jobs are often low paid and repetitive in nature. As number of female workers in the informal sector in India has gone up considerably, it implies employment opportunity for them in the formal sector have become restricted. On account of easy availability of low paid labour in the informal sector, there is an every possibility of more and more economic activity in the sector. The informal sector studies in the developing countries reveal that informal sector always considers as employment generating sector although the earnings from the sector has been often found less than that offered by the formal sector employment. So far as determinants of the earnings of informal sector are concerned the human capital theory suggests that effect of educational attainment and work experience on the earnings in the informal sector is predicted to be insignificant and workers are expected to exhibit a flat profile of earnings across age groups and earnings are positively related to workers age (House 1984: 297).

It is found that among all categories in the informal sector, earnings of domestic workers are lowest and their problems are many. They are being employed generally for household tasks which include washing utensils and clothes, fetching water, sweeping and cleaning house along with a few outdoor tasks like irregular marketing, grocery shopping, ration drawing even childcare activity. Clearly, one of the main differences between paid and unpaid domestic work is that former involves following a work routine, which is imposed by the employer's order rather than evolved for oneself (Cock 1989). In fact, many of these women are looking after more than one household but spend more time and work far more for their employer's than work in their own household. In many studies the focus has been on women's labour participation in agricultural and allied activities often erroneously considered to be only form of paid work available to the women of lower strata. In fact, in many rural areas female labourers work as domestic worker, often combining this employment with agricultural work on a seasonal and even daily wage basis (Kothari 1991). Hence, domestic work contributes a substantive type of employment and generation of earnings for many women.

OBJECTIVES

Over last few decades, there have been a rapid growth in the number of women employed in India with majority of them being engaged in informal sector of the economy where jobs are often low paid and repetitive. As the number of female workers in the informal sector in India has gone up considerably, it implies employment opportunities for them in the formal sector have become restricted. On account of easy availability of low paid labour in the informal sector, there is every possibility of more and more economic activities in this sector. Therefore, an attempt has been made in this study to trace out the problems associated with the process of women participation as well as the manner in which workingwomen's lives in the informal sector in West Bengal are being affected by the process of economic development and social change. The objectives of the study are to examine the level of women labour participation in domestic services. An effort has been made to reveal the socio-economic conditions of paid domestic workers in State. It has also been tried to examine the general nature of working conditions of women domestic workers, their special problems and how they combine wage work with domestic responsibilities in the State.

METHOD AND LIMITATION

The study of women at work in the informal sector with special reference to female domestic workers in West Bengal is an empirical one. The study is based on survey research technique. The various informations on 200 sample female domestic workers in the informal sector have been gathered from extensive survey. The data were collected through face-to-face interview technique. Since working women in informal sector in the State constitutes a heterogeneous group, stratified sampling method has been undertaken while collecting the sample workers. The required information has been gathered from extensive survey of field investigation and primary data collection was carried out by obtaining individual responses to questionnaires. This study, however, is not free from its limitations. The data is based on the respondents estimate and memory recall. Since most of the women workers in informal sector are illiterate, their inability to provide precise information put in trouble in generalizing the case. Some respondents were unwilling to disclose their exact earning and they had no idea regarding their expenditure patterns. These limitations may have affected the survey result to some extent. Despite these limitations, the researcher has taken utmost care in analyzing the problems.

PAID AND UNPAID DOMESTIC WORKS

Two types of domestic work can be found in practice namely, paid domestic work and unpaid domestic work. While a maid is employed for doing sundry household tasks on the basis of agreed wage payment, the daily activities performed by the maid in the respective employer's household may be termed as paid domestic work. On the other hand, the time spent by a male or female folk in different activities of own household may be termed as unpaid domestic work. Paid household work is always visible, but unpaid one is often invisible. A United Nations (1991) report on women's work patterns based on surveys made across countries of the world gives a summary of women's devotion of time to both paid and unpaid economic activity. The findings are as under:

- Women spend more of their time working than men folk in all developed and developing regions except northern America and Australia where the working hours are almost equal.
- In developing countries, women spend more time in the labour force than their household work. Men, by contrast, are spending less amount of time working in the labour force than before in all developed regions and slightly increasing amounts of time in housework in northern America, Australia and Western Europe.
- In Africa, Asia and the Pacific, women work as on average 12-13 hours more than men per week.
- Men in developing regions generally do less household chores than men in the developed regions.

- Women everywhere in the world have nearly total responsibility for housework. While men 'help out' women retain the responsibility of housework.

Since the unpaid domestic workers do not manage all household tasks, often they have to employ an additional paid domestic worker in their household. The demand for or dependency on paid domestic maids among middle class families is on the rise because of the following reasons:

- Men spend very little time on their daily indoor household activities and a slow increase in household work by men (Juster 1985, Ramu 1987, Spitze 1988, Thompson and Walker 1989). Hence, it becomes impossible to do all necessary household tasks by an unpaid female folk.
- While woman of a household is employed, her husband does not show any substantial increase in the amount of family work they do (Kammaeyer 1987). Obviously, dependency on paid domestic workers increases.

PROBLEM AT WORK PLACE

The general problems faced by the female domestic workers at work place are as under:

- The domestic workers are not satisfied with their present wages and they expect more. It is true that the wage levels of domestic maids are much less than not only what they need, but also lower than their male counterparts who often do almost comparable type of work.
- The workers often express their grievances for imposing extra work burden by the employers while guests come. The extra money for that additional work is not sufficient. A lump sum amount is paid for extra work. Often, the employer does not pay anything.

- Few employers have a tendency to deduct wage for absence in work.
- The employers do not permit any extra leave. As a result, they have to attend work regularly leaving any urgent personal necessity.
- Many workers face sexual harassment by their male employers. Verbal sexual harassment by the male employers is some thing that is generally very common. This is one of those problems at work place that only women face and it is probably one of the few problems that may be perpetuated by male employer.
- Most of the workers being less educated, the awareness to form a union is lacking among them. As there is no such domestic workers' unions formed across the country, they cannot raise their voice against employers' negative attitude.
- The real wages in the form of food, cloth etc. is not sufficient. Sometimes quality of food provided by the employer is inferior.
- Often nature of work may vary from one day to another or volume of work rises day by day in the employers' house. Then the workers have to do all tasks with initial agreed wages. The employers do not offer any extra wages for increasing workload. On the other hand, workers do not protest because of getting fired.
- So far as the annual increment of wages is concerned, a few domestic workers enjoy the benefit.

WORK AND WAGES

More or less all middle and upper class people employ preferably female domestic worker in their households. The female domestic workers can be categorized as *thika* workers, full time workers and residential workers. The *thika* (piece rate) workers serve for 3-4 hours a day in a household. They work in 2-3 houses daily. However, number of households to be served by thika workers largely depends on their efficiency and capability to work. On the other hand, the full time workers serve in a single household for maximum duration of 8–10 hours daily which includes a part of idle time. The employers normally provide them one time meal. Often, thika workers demand for one time meal while there is a heavy workload. The residential workers stay at employer's house and they are provided two time meal. The residential workers do all works of the employer's household. Apart from these three types of domestic maids, another type of domestic worker may be found. They are part time 'occasional or emergency' workers who serve for a few days on a purely temporary basis when any emergency arises in a household. They generally work in the present employer's neighbour's household for a very short duration.

The tasks performed by all types of domestic workers are almost same. They perform a bunch of work such as cleaning utensils, sweeping and cleaning rooms, washing clothes, fetching water etc. The cooking is generally delegated to the efficient workers. This skilled task is not assigned to lower class workers, because higher caste employers do not allow schedule caste or schedule tribe women to enter their kitchen. However, caste is not a matter for other household tasks. More over, some allied tasks are to be carried out by the domestic maids namely, minding little children, daily marketing, looking after house etc., but their number is small. Therefore, the activities performed by paid domestic workers are similar to those carried out within their own household, although specific tasks and ways of carrying them out may vary. One domestic maid described her workday as under:

I come to *Bowdi*'s house at 7 am daily. While I reach at Bowdi's house, she gives me a cup of tea and biscuit.

Then I go to fetch water from nearby drinking water tap. The containers are heavy and often I have to make double trip. I can meet my friends at the tap and we interact until our return. Every day I have to stand in a long queue for fetching water. Sometimes Bowdi shouts at me do not waste so much time at tap, there is a lot of sundry work to do. After getting back from tap I have to assist Bowdi regarding breakfast and food preparation, because *Dada* goes to office at 10 am. Then I clean house and wash clothes. I have to wash 6-10 clothes daily. Then I clean bathroom. After they have eaten, I wash dishes and utensils. In most of the days, I do no eat there. I go home at 12 noon with my food and cook for my family. I again come back at 3 pm and again go to fetch water. After washing utensils and sweeping the rooms, I watch movie on the television at Bowdi's house. I go back my house at 5 pm. On my way home, I collect firewood. I earn Rs. 300 per month, but the amount is insufficient for the survival of my family.

One domestic worker complained that I have to wake up early in the morning to prepare food for my family. I leave my children unfed so that I can arrive at doctor's house to wash and dress his children. Most of the domestic maids carry out all domestic tasks except cooking. It is generally thought that cooking involves some skill and expertise, moreover being a time consuming process, therefore cannot be done efficiently by a domestic worker. In lieu of cooking in the employer's household, they can serve in more than two households at a time.

Domestic workers are often to do tasks for other members of their employers' guests, particularly during special occasions. During this time, domestic workers can carry out necessary preparations together with other workers. Although, this involves a lot of work but many workers enjoy the change from daily monotonous routine work that they are to perform and it is one of the few occasions while they can work together. However, one woman described the problems faced at such time:

I had to work for the whole day a week because of *Didi*'s wedding. All they gave me was little extra money and a *sari*. My children came with me, but they were simply neglected. The employer's extra money does not help with all that work.

Domestic workers carry out other tasks, which are not linked with domestic workers. Domestic maids are often sent as messenger from one woman to another. While for example, a neighbouring household requires a maid, the employers of the household already having worker sends her domestic worker to persuade her fellow friend to work for other. This role as messenger provides the workers with a degree of power as the employer may depend on her for additional need of worker in future.

Since domestic workers are required to work extra hours, they become unable to maintain their own domestic responsibilities. As a result, their husbands and other household members ask for negotiation against extra demand of the employers. The worker(s) addressed:

The employers want us to work more particularly during special occasions, but our husbands get angry. One day my employer wanted me to stay and work in the evening. Initially, I did not agree because I am to cook for my family. I required money for my child's education, so I did the work. Sometimes my husband gets angry because of serving extra hours for the employers. While I work overtime, then I do not have enough hours for looking after my own household.

Thus, domestic workers have to combine different types of work in order to survive and must organize their time with a view to meeting all duties properly.

So far as the wage is concerned, it is based on the nature of work, number of members in employer's household, size of the house or number of rooms, time to be spent etc. Wages paid for performing allied activities is generally higher than usual household work. Among all types of domestic workers, thika worker is paid least. The residential workers get more wages in cash in addition to their daily real wages than a thika maid. The wages of full time and residential workers do not differ so, but latter enjoy more real wages than former. Besides, part time occasional or emergency workers always expect high wage from the employers and their total earnings at the end of the part time job become lucrative as compared to their average earnings. Apart from the cash wages, domestic maids received new clothes and festival grant in cash.

The wages of domestic workers may vary from one region to another. It is found that rate of wages in semi urban areas are comparatively lower than urban areas. This is because, supply of domestic workers in semi urban areas is often more than their demand and sometimes workers belonging to semi urban areas have no bargaining capacity. However, still the wages of domestic workers are low in comparison with other workers in the informal sector.

SURVEY FINDINGS

The field survey on 200 female domestic workers randomly selected from 200 households in West Bengal. The following is the general findings of the survey.

It is surprising to note that few of the domestic workers emigrated from Bangladesh. Although the reported percentage was not significant, but their number is on the rise. The number of native domestic workers was 183. Therefore, domestic workers and maids have tended to focus on the international migration of women labourers.

The general educational standard of the female domestic workers was very low. It has been observed that 89 per cent of the workers were illiterate. Only 11 per cent of the workers had schooling experience. Out of 11 per cent, 9.5 per cent had primary education and 1.5 per cent had education beyond the primary level. Only one woman had passed class VIII standard.

The nature of employment of all domestic workers did not identical. Someone preferred to work as thika maid, but other might like to serve as residential or full time worker. It is found that majority of the domestic workers preferred to work as thika workers on the assumption of more earnings. It has been found that 81 per cent of the workers served as thika labour, while 6 per cent of the workers stayed in the employers' households. Thika and full time domestic maids lived in nearby locality, but most of the residential maids migrated from other districts or villages. Out of 12 residential maids, 7 were from different regions of West Bengal. A good number of employers preferred to employ adolescent maids, because they could easily be directed and motivated for household work. Their probability to leave the employer's household was also minimal.

The recruitment of the domestic workers may be done either through employers' own effort or through workers' own effort. Sometimes, would be employers' neighbour's effort as well as fellow workers' effort play a vital role in recruitment of domestic workers. In fact, direct recruitment through employers' own effort constituted 36.5 per cent. It is observed that as far as the recruitment of domestic maids was concerned workers' own effort and their fellows' effort constituted 49 per cent. While would be employers' neighbour's effort was only 14.5 per cent. Generally part time maids were employed with the help of neighbour.

Two types of domestic maids can be identified from the survey. One group of workers was not breadwinners of their family, but willing to serve as domestic workers for income supplementation. On the other hand, most of the domestic maids were working to earn their livelihood.

The first group of workers started working mainly after giving birth of first child. According to them, they preferred and enjoyed the work. But most of the respondents were forced to do this job to feed their family. According to them, there was no alternative way to earn money with such a little education.

Economic compulsion was the main reason behind taking the job as domestic maids (91.5 per cent). 5.5 per cent of the workers reported that they had chosen the job for supporting their husband. A few per cent of workers served for independent income (3 per cent). There was no worker in the findings who worked for passing out idle time. A majority percentage of workers had to travel on foot to reach at work place (78.72 per cent). 14.36 per cent of domestic maids reported that they availed their husband's *rickshaw* to arrive at work place. Only 6.92 per cent of the workers used other mode of transpiration like bus or train.

The workers had to serve for their own household also. The thika and full time maids had to simultaneously manage their own family. The table 2.1 shows the level of participation of domestic maids in own household work.

It is found that apart from the employer' sundry household works, maids had to do a lot of tasks for their own family. The domestic workers had nearly total responsibility for own housework. It is also noticed that their husbands spent a little time on the large bulk of daily indoor activities like washing clothes and utensils, water collection and cooking. Hence, majority of the household work was to be carried out by the maid herself.

It is rational that maids should get refreshment like tea, bread etc. and minimum one time food at work place irrespective of their nature of work. Among the respondent workers, 50.5 per cent enjoyed refreshment only and 36.5 per cent got food either once or twice a day depending upon their nature of employment. 13 per cent of the workers did not get any type of refreshment and food at work place.

The domestic workers had grievances against the employers. 18 per cent of the workers reported that they were considered as *Naukrani* (a derogatory local term to indicate the maidservant) in the employers' households. However, many employers treated their domestic maids as a family member (65.5 per cent). A few employers also commanded excessively over the workers (5 per cent). Besides, the maids faced other type of gender specific forms of discrimination and oppressions at their work place. A severe problem women workers faced was that of sexual harassment by the male employers (11.5 per cent).

The extent of trustworthiness of employers was not always satisfactory. 51 per cent of the maids reported that their employers trusted on them moderately. The high trustworthiness among the employers was only 4.5 per cent. Some employers had no trustworthiness at all (6 per cent).

Sometimes the workers had to participate in doing allied activities in the employer's household. These were in addition to the regular household tasks. Daily marketing, ration drawing, childcare activities etc. were often found to be performed by the domestic maids where in general husband and wife both were employed. The percentage of the workers involved in such activities is 16.5. The workers complained that they had not been paid enough for doing these allied tasks. Often they had been provided a lump sum amount at the end of every month. Instead of doing such activities, they preferred to earn by serving another households. They did not really like such activities. This is why 83.5 per cent of the workers did not take participation in such activities.

The number of the household to be served by the workers largely depends on the physical capability of the individual worker. It is found that young adults served in more than two households at a time (52 per cent), while old aged maids served in a single household. The middle aged maids preferred to work as thika worker and old ones like to serve as full time maid. It is found that 13 per cent of the workers served in more than three households daily.

Very often the contribution that a female worker makes to the family determines her status in the household. The earnings of the workers are considered to be right fully at disposal of the household. But there is no or a very little concept of women's autonomy to control over their own earnings. It has been found that most of the female domestic workers contributed to their household in the range of Rs. 200 and Rs. 300 per month (82 per cent). 5.5 per cent of the respondents had a contribution of Rs. 300 to Rs. 400, while 3 per cent of them did not contribute at all.

Few workers were very much concerned about the potentiality of savings. They saved a part of their earnings either at post office or at home. It is interestingly found that a few employers convinced the workers to go for saving. A few maids deposited a certain amount in the post office every month thinking for the future (2.0 per cent). However, majority of the workers had no any saving potentiality (86.5 per cent) although they were eager to save, but a limited fund did not permit.

Table 2.2 shows daily work profile of female domestic maids of various age groups. The table is arranged taking into account of average activities performed by them. Column 2 reveals activities of an adolescent girl. Column 3 shows activities of a maid in middle age group and column 4 discloses a day of a woman in the old age group. The daily tight schedule of the domestic workers has been presented in table 2.2.

Table 2.1
Level of Participation in Own Household Task by Domestic Workers

Household tasks	*Self*	*Husband / other members*	*Jointly*
Washing clothes and utensils	176 (93.62)	02 (1.06)	10 (5.32)
Water collection	185 (98.40)	01 (0.54)	02 (1.06)
Fuel collection	105 (55.85)	60 (31.91)	23 (12.24)
Food preparation	188 (100.00)	0 (0)	0 (0)
Maintenance of house	57 (30.32)	71 (37.77)	60 (31.91)
Childcare	176 (93.62)	08 (4.26)	04 (2.12)

Figures in the parentheses are percentages.
Only thika and full time workers were considered.

Table 2.2
Daily Work Profile of Female Domestic Workers

Time	*Young age group*	*Middle age group*	*Old age group*
5.00 am	—	Rises	Rises
5.30 am	—	Fetches water and cleans own house	Fetches water for family
6.00 am	Rises	Feeds children	Prepares breakfast for family
6.30 am	Takes breakfast	Prepares breakfast for family	Attends work place–1 and takes breakfast
7.00 am	Goes to work place and does domestic tasks	Goes to work place–1 and washes utensils, clothes, cleans rooms	Does domestic work at work place
8.00 am	Helps in cooking at work place	Takes breakfast at work place	Prepares food at work place
10.00 am	Does other work at work place	Goes to work place–2 and does work	Goes to work place–2 andprepares food

Time	*Young age group*	*Middle age group*	*Old age group*
12.00 noon	Returns home	Attends work place–3 and does work	Returns home
1.30 pm	Helps mother at home	Returns home and cook for the family	Takes rest
2.30 pm	Takes food at work place	Takes rest	Takes food at work place and does some work
3.30 pm	Washes utensils andsweeps rooms	Washes utensils and sweeps rooms	Returns home
5.00 pm	Returns home	Returns home and washes clothes	Interacts with neighbour
7.00 pm	Helps mother at home	Prepares food and feeds the children	Takes food and goes to bed
8.00 pm	Takes food	Takes food	—
9.00 pm	Goes to bed	Goes to bed	—

SUMMARY

The demand for women domestic help among middle and upper strata people in West Bengal is generally fulfilled from native women and often domestic service contributes a substantive form of employment and generation of earnings for many poor women in the State. The domestic tasks can be classified as paid domestic work and unpaid domestic work. The paid domestic workers generally perform a series of household tasks such as cleaning utensils, sweeping and cleaning rooms, washing clothes, fetching water etc. However, the cooking is assigned to the expert workers. The wages of the female domestic workers are very low compared to other workers in the informal sector. The domestic workers enjoy both money wages as well as real wages. The female domestic workers have to face a lot of problems at the work place which include low level of wage, a minimal pay or no pay for extra work, absence of leave facility, sexual harassment by male employer etc. These problems can never be overcome until the concept of unionism is developed among the female domestic workers. The economic compulsion is the main hardship for taking the job as domestic workers. The general educational status of the female domestic workers in the district is not satisfactory. The workers contribute a lion part of their earnings to the family and few of them have saving potentials too. Since wages of the female domestic workers are very low, they have been worst exploited. The female domestic workers are subject to variety of exploitations starting from low wages to maltreatment and sexual harassment by the employer. However, with a view to improving the working conditions of female domestic workers the following suggestions are recommended:

First, fixing wages to keep pace with other paid work in the informal sector.

Secondly, providing support service like day meal to all domestic workers irrespective of their nature of work.

Thirdly, providing the workers some degree of flexibility in working hours.

Fourthly, minimizing degree of command over the workers by the employers and imposing acceptable workload to the workers.

Fifthly, building up proper understanding between workers and employers over worker's failure to attend at work.

Sixthly, setting up formal domestic workers unions, which can look after their interests.

Seventhly, providing equitable extra wages for extra workload due to arrival of employer's guests on holidays and festivals. Eighthly, providing annual incremental benefit to all workers. Ninthly, providing minimum leave facilities to the workers.

Lastly, passing out legislations for the welfare of the workers.

REFERENCES

Cock, J. (1989), *Maids and Madams: Domestic Workers under Apartheid*. The Women's Press, London.

House, W.J. (1984),Nairobi's Informal Sector: Dynamic Entrepreneurs or Surplus Labour? *Economic Development and Cultural Change*, 32 (2): 277-302.

Juster, F.T. (1985),Investments of Time by Men and Women. In F.T. Juster and F.P. Stafford (eds.). *Time, Goods and Well-being*. University of Michigan, Survey Research Centre.

Kammaeyer, K.C.W. (1987), *Marriage and Family: A Foundation of Personal Decisions*. Allyn and Bacon, New York.

Kothari, U. (1991), *Women's Work and Rural Transformation in India*. Unpublished Ph.D. Thesis, University of Edinburgh.

Ramu, G.N. (1987), Indian Husbands: Their Role Perceptions and Performance in Single and Dual Earner Families. *Journal of Marriage and the Family*, 49: 903-915.

Sarkar, S. (2004), Theorising in Informal Sector: Concept and Context. *Social Action*, 54 (4): 359-373.

Spitz, G. (1998), Women's Employment and Family Relations: A Review. *Journal of Marriage and the Family,* 50: 595-618.

Thomson, L. and Walker, A.J. (1989), Gender in Families: Women and Men in Marriage, Work and Parenthood. *Journal of Marriage and the Family*, 51: 845-871.

United Nations. 1991. *The World's Women 1970-1990.* New York: UN.

Chapter - 3

Women in Bidi Rolling

INTRODUCTION

Bidi tobacco is the most important non-virginia tobacco produced in India. It occupies 25 to 30 per cent of the total area under tobacco in the country, while in terms of production its share is around 30 to 35 per cent. This type of tobacco accounts for about 50 per cent of the total production of all types of non-virginia tobacco in the country. Bidi is typically Indian. Bidis are also smoked in neighbouring countries of Bangladesh, Nepal, Pakistan, Sri Lanka, Singapore and Malaysia. By far, the largest produced of bidi is in India, accounting for about 85 per cent of the total world production. In manufacture of bidis, the industry is using annually about 150 million kilogram of bidi tobacco and 30 million kilograms of bidi wrapper leaves. The annual production of bidi is presently estimated to be more than 55,000 crore pieces and sales of bidi are ten times higher than cigarette sales. Bidi industry is essentially a cottage industry providing gainful employment to more than 30 lakh of mostly rural population. This industry is basically rural oriented, labour intensive and also makes significant contribution to revenue to the government. During 1987-88 all tobacco products contributed to the National Exchequer on excise revenue of Rs. 1,686.24 crore, of which the contribution from bidis alone accounted for Rs 169.22 crore, while during 2000-2001 the total excise duty collected from bidi industry was Rs 354 crore. The location of the industry is decided more by the presence of cheap labour and availability of tendu leaves used in bidi rolling (Directorate of Tobacco Development 1990: 36).

Bidi rolling is an agro-based labour intensive industry with an employment size next only to agriculture and the handloom sector (Government of India 1995). The existing studies on the socio economic conditions of bidi workers in different parts of the country reveal that their continuing struggle for survival even while sustaining in this activity in spite of low wages, irregular employment and steady exploitation by middle men and agent, lack of credit, education and medical facilities and neglect in government policies (Avachat 1978; Mishra 2000). There are several studies on socio-economic conditions of bidi workers and their problems in Indian context. These studies have dealt with the problems in availing benefits of social security measures like weekly holidays, provision for annual leave, maternity leave for women workers, sick leave and medical benefits. Further, they have emphasised on the status of working and living conditions, poverty indebtedness and sexual exploitation (Government of India 1994-95; Mohandas 1980; Mohandas and Praveen Kumar 1992). There are various studies conducted at regional level to address the socio-economic conditions of bidi workers. These studies have mainly highlighted on low wages, working hours, indebtedness, illiteracy, health conditions, role of trade unions and problems of contract system, both in rural and urban areas (Saravanan 2001; Srinivasan 1999). At the national level, studies conducted by the government concluded that welfare measures have failed to produce the expected result (Government of India 1981; Government of India 1994-95).

In India, bidi manufacturing is not uniform in terms of capital invested, number of persons employed and the size of bidi and also in terms of concentration. There are a few units in the organised sector, but most of the units are in the unorganised cottage sector. No fixed promises are required for bidi making unless it is other than home working. The only tools that are required for bidi rolling include a pair of scissors for cutting the wrapper, a small hand knife and trays to keep the raw materials. The process is very simple but does require much skill for neat and even turn out (Giriappa 1987).

Under the contract system of employment in bidi industry, the trademark owner provides bidi tobacco and tendu leaves to the contractor, who on receiving the materials makes bidis by directly employing labourers or by distributing the raw materials to the home workers. The latter form of arrangement is common where in there is women who primarily roll bidis with the help of the male members and children. However, in some cases, the workers may receive the raw materials directly from the manufacturers and supply bidis directly to them. In few cases, it is not unusual to find bidi making being carried out in tiny scale. A family may roll out and sell few thousand per day. Moreover, up to a certain level of production, tiny scale bidi making is kept out of the excise preview by the government, which encourages small-scale production.

SCOPE AND METHODOLOGY

The objectives of the study are to examine to socio-economic profile of the female bidi workers along with their perceive health status. However, the paper also delves into economic significance and employment pattern in bidi industry, appalling condition of the bidi workers as well as work and wages of bidi labourers. The study was conducted in West Bengal having a good number of bidi industry and household/non-household activities. The data were collected through face to face interview of 200 female workers. The various information on female bidi workers have been gathered from survey of field investigation and primary data collection was done by obtaining individual responses to questionnaires. The stratified random sampling method has been undertaken while collecting the sample workers.

ECONOMIC SIGNIFICANCE OF BIDI INDUSTRY

The following table presents the generation of gross value in different sub-sectors of bidi industry including domestic consumption and exports. The total value generation of Rs. 6,110 crore by the industry is accounted for by different sub-sectors as:

Table 3.1
Gross Value Generated by Bidi Industry
(Rupees in crore)

Cultivator	*Processor*	*Manufacturer*	*Wholesaler*	*Retailer*	*Total*
329 (6%)	129 (2%)	5,064 (83%)	104 (2%)	484 (8%)	6,110

Source: Computed from Indian Market Research Bureau Report on Cigarette and Bidi Industry–A Comparative Status [1996].

Roughly one-third of the value generated by the bidi industry flows into supplier sectors. The magnitude of the direct dependence of a large number of non-tobacco sectors on the bidi industry is, therefore, considerable.

The table 3.2 shows that value addition is more than double the input cost in bidi industry. The gross value added within the industry is Rs. 4,122 crore. Therefore, importance of bidi industry in respect of contribution to the gross domestic product is significant. Of greater significance is perhaps the per man-day contribution to the gross domestic product as well as the per stick value addition generated by the industry (Tobacco News 1997: 5).

Table 3.2
Distribution of Gross Value Addition Bidi Industry
(Rupees in crore)

Gross Value Generated	6,110
Input Cost	1,988 (33%)
Gross Value Added by Bidi Industry by way of wages, interest, rent and profit earned	4,122 (67%)

Source: Computed from Indian Market Research Bureau Report on Cigarette and Industry–A Comparative Status [1996].

The foreign exchange earning from export of bidis over the past three years reveals that during 1998-99 the value of foreign exchange earning was 7.58 million US $, during 1999-2001 the same was 7.43 million US $ (Table 3.3). Thus, the total value of foreign exchange earning during the period 1998-2001 was 23.70 million US $ and total quantity of bidis exported during the same period was 3,134 tones (Table 3.3).

Table 3.3
Exports of Bidis

Year	*Quantity (Tones)*	*Value (US $ Million)*
1998-99	998	7.58
1999-2000	1,174	8.69
2000-2001	962	7.43

Source: Directorate General of Commercial Intelligence and Statistics and Tobacco Board.

BIDI INDUSTRY: A MAJOR EMPLOYER

The figures on employment in bidi industry during 1993-94 to 1996-97 were around 4.4 million (Rajasekhar and Sreedhar 2002: 4023). At present, the bidi industry generates a considerable employment, aggregating to a total of about 44,11,275 persons. The following table illustrates the number of persons engaged as bidi workers in the different states of the country.

Table 3.4
Employment in Bidi Industry

Name of the State	*Total number of bidi workers estimated at present*
Madhya Pradesh	7,50,000
Andhra Pradesh	6,25,050
Tamil Nadu	6,20,950
West Bengal	4,97,458
Uttar Pradesh	4,50,000
Bihar	3,91,500
Karnataka	3,60,876
Maharastra	2,56,000
Orissa	1,60,000
Kerala	1,36,416
Rajasthan	1,00,000
Gujarat	50,000
Assam	7,725
Tripura	5,000
Total	44,11,275

Source: Tobacco Institute of India: A Summary of Questions and Answers in Parliament, The Golden Leaf in Parliament[2001].

Besides, the industry generated a total of 13,106 lakh man-days. The break down in percentage terms is as under:

Table 3.5
Man-days Deployed in Bidi Industry
(Rupees in lakh)

Cultivator	*Processor*	*Manufacturer*	*Distributor*	*Total*
415 (3%)	88 (1%)	8,892 (68%)	3,711 (28%)	13,106

Source: Computed from Indian Market Research Bureau Report on Cigarette and Bidi Industry–A Comparative Status [1996].

Thus, the bidi industry employs a very large work force at the aggregate level, besides representing substantial employment across each sub-sector. Both in terms of man-days as well as in terms of number of persons employed, the industry wields tremendous socio-economic importance.

BIDI WORKERS IN INDIA

As per latest estimates there are about 44.11 lakh bidi workers in the country. The Labour Bureau (Ministry of Labour) has conducted a sample survey on the working and living conditions of the workers in the bidi industry in 1995. According to the survey, 65.9 per cent women workers and one per cent children are engaged in bidi making.

The government has introduced various welfare measures for the bidi workers through the Bidi Workers Welfare Fund Act, 1976. These include financial assistance for their housing, healthcare, educational needs for children and recreational needs. Besides, the Minimum Wages Act was enacted in 1948 to protect the interest of the workers engaged mostly in the informal sector. Under the provisions of the Act, both central and state governments are the appropriate authority to fix, revise and enforce payment of minimum wages in scheduled employments falling under their respective jurisdictions. Bidi making is a scheduled employment only in the state sphere. The wages are generally on piece rate basis. Hence, erosion of bidi sales could lead to reduce work per person and should not result in unemployment. Research has also shown that on 22 per cent of households involved in bidi making are fully dependent on bidi income and bidi work is largely a supplementary income among most of the women.

The appalling condition of bidi workers despite the government passing several legislations for their welfare is also worth mentioning. Women constitute a majority of the bidi industry's work force. Since most women bidi workers operate from their homes, they are isolated from the rest of the industry workforce and therefore are easy targets for exploitation. There are a large number of cases where acute poverty has forced bidi rolling women to mortgage their children to repay debts (Tobacco News 1997:7). Employers consistently deny minimum wages to bidi workers even the government has fixed these for them. The incidence of child labour is also significant in bidi industry. In some districts of Tamil Nadu women have pledged their yet to be born children to bidi employers in order to repay debt.

However, the bidi workers in India have been facing the following problems:

(a) Wide disparity in minimum wages.

(b) Limited implementation of even statutory social security schemes like provident fund and insurance.

(c) Short supply of raw materials and non-payment for rejected bidis.

(d) Predominance of illness like tuberculosis, asthma, and problems of eyesight.

(e) Deprivation of children due to lack of educational inputs.

The aspirations of bidi workers for better standard of living and education, coupled with improved economic conditions and employment opportunities will drive them to shift to better jobs (Tobacco News 1996: 7).

WORK AND WAGES

The manufacturing process of bidi consists of rolling, sorting, drying, labeling and packing. The female labour is preferred for rolling bidis, while sorting, drying, labeling and packing activities are carried out by the male workers. Before rolling, the tendu wrapper leaves are soaked in water over night and cut into suitable pieces for wrapping blended tobacco mix. The size of leaves, nature of tobacco blend may vary according to the different trademarks. The process of rolling comprises in taking a small quantity of tobacco flake on the wrapper kept ready for the purpose, spreading the flakes evenly and then rolling the wrapper between fingers diagonally to give a conical shape. A piece of cotton thread is tied toward the smoking end. The edges of the wrapper pieces are placed partially inside this end and the flattened smoking tip remains partly open. The broad end is closed by folding the open edges inward. The size of the bidi may vary from 5 cm to 6 cm in length as per different manufacture practices. An average roller can make two to three bidis per minute, though some experienced and skilled hands can roll even four to six bidis. Average daily working hours for the worker is fairly ranging from 6 to 8 and number of bidis rolled by an average worker per week is about 5,500. While rolling process is over, the bidis are packed in a bundle of usually twenty-five and brought to the principal employer or contractor. The workers have to deposit bidis following the instructions of the employers. Generally, all bidis are collected from the workers twice or thrice in a week. One bidi worker traces out her workday as follows:

I collect bidi leaves and tobacco from my employer twice in a week. I can roll about 6,000 bidis per week. I have to work sincerely for fulfilling my expected level. I wake up early and prepare breakfast. I begin rolling at 7 am and carry on the activity up to 10 am. During this period of time, I have to roll about 500 to 600 bidis daily. Then, I go for other household work and cook for my family. In the evening, I have to take care of my children after rolling 100 to 200 bidis side by side. I devote as much as 7 to 8 hours daily for the work. I enjoy the work because it provides me certain amount of independence in addition to money wages.

The bidi workers are employed by the principal employer or by the contractor. Under factory employment system, the trademark owner supplies bidi tobacco and tendu leaves to the factory workers who roll bidis at their own premises and supply the finished product timely to the trademark owner, while under contract system of employment, which is most widespread, the principal employer supplies the raw materials to the contractors who on receiving the raw materials employ labourers and supply the finished product to the principal employer. The contractors have to keep the particulars about the workers and they will have to report to the principal employer time to time about the quantum of output produced by the workers. Besides, the workers have to account for raw materials received from the contractors by rolling the stipulated quantity of bidis. Usually, 500 grams leaves and 300 grams tobacco are supplied for rolling 1,000 bidis. Sometimes, the workers have to buy extra quantity of raw materials from outside to set right the deficiency. If workers roll sub-standard size of bidis, they have to make good for the same out of their own pocket. The workers have some genuine grievances against the contractors. One bidi worker complained:

Often contractors provide us inferior quality of tendu leaves, which is inadequate for rolling stipulated number of bidis. In every week, I have to purchase raw materials from the market at a high price in order to meet the deficiency. The rejection of two or three bidis out of a bunch of twenty-five is the common practice of the contractor.

The wage rate for bidi rolling largely varies from one manufacturer to another. The principal employers or manufacturers after making discussion with the concerned trade union settle the wage rate. So there is a possibility of revision of wage rate every three to four years after. In bidi rolling, female and girl child workers are mostly preferred because of the limitation of alternative job opportunities for them and moreover, they can be easily exploited by the contractors in paying a lower wage rate. The wage rate for the factory workers in West

Bengal largely varies from Rs. 30 to Rs. 33.50 per 1,000 bidis, while contract workers are paid of Rs. 24 to Rs. 28. Most of the workers have experienced to incur on average expenses of Rs. 1.50 to Rs. 2 per 1,000 bidis out of own pocket due to deficiency of raw materials and rejection of defective bidis which turn into a further decrease in wage rate. Apart from the regular money wage, the factory workers are provided other benefits like provident fund contribution and ex-gratia. Besides these, children of bidi workers get scholarship for study and bidi workers welfare fund is being utilized for the benefit of the labour force.

REVELATIONS OF STUDY

The field survey on 200 female bidi workers randomly chosen from 200 households from West Bengal. The general findings of the survey are as follows: It is found that the main concentration of female bidi workers was in the age group of 25-34 (41.5 per cent). At the same time 11per cent of the women workers were virtually child labour in the sense that they were in the age of below 14. 24.5 per cent of the workers were in the age group of 15-24, while only six workers were found to be age above 45. Usually, old female workers did not engage in bidi rolling because of their eyesight problems.

It is further observed that among the bidi workers, the illiterates constituted 47 per cent. 53 per cent of the women had gone to school. Of the total respondents, 30.5 per cent had the primary education. 22.5 per cent of the workers had the education beyond the primary level. It is interestingly found that young adults had more educational status than the other women. Majority of child workers were school goers too.

The bidi workers may be recruited by the principal employer or contractor. The survey discloses that 48 per cent of the total workers were employed by the principal employers or manufactures, while 52 per cent of the workers were recruited by the contractors. The demand for contract employment was on the rise because of limited opportunity to work as direct factory labour.

The economic compulsion was the main reasons of the workers behind taking up bidi rolling as their livelihood (58 per cent). However, there were a small percentage (4.5 per cent) of the workers, mostly the wives from middle class families, who entered the job market for passing out idle time. Besides, 6.5 per cent of the workers, mostly child labourers, entered the labour force for meeting own educational expenses. The vast majority of the female bidi workers joined the workforce for supporting their child's educational expenses.

It is found that an average worker could roll about 5,500 bidis per week. 53.5 per cent of the workers rolled 4,001-5,000 bidis per week, while 30 per cent of the workers made 5,001-7,000 bidis. Most of the child workers had capacity to make 3,000-4,000 bidis. Generally, young adults group rolled 5,001-7,000 bidis. Nineteen workers were found to roll more than 7,000 bidis.

The survey shows the responses about work experiences of the female bidi workers in bidi rolling. The respondents were asked to recall the age at which they began rolling. 14 per cent of the workers reported that they had been working for less than 3 years, while 49 per cent of the workers had an experience of 8-15 years. 16 per cent of the workers had more than 16 years experience. The majority of middle age group workers joined the labour force at the age of 10-15 years old.

The female bidi rollers were affected by the tobacco flakes and tendu wrapper leaves they handle day in and day out. It is found that some health related problems like tuberculosis, asthma and eyesight problems increased with age and number of years work. 32 per cent of the women had no major health problems except the problems like headache, shoulder pain, leg pain etc. All the rest had faced acute health problems due to inhalation of tobacco dust. 44.5 per cent of the workers had been suffering from asthma, while 21per cent of the workers had eyesight problems. Five workers had faced problem like tuberculosis.

It is clearly evident from the survey that 14 per cent of the female bidi workers possessed some agricultural land, 28 per cent of the workers owned a radio set and 4 per cent of the bidi workers had an audiotape. Only nine women possessed a watch. As far as the additional furniture was concerned, 19 per cent of the workers were found to have wooden chairs, tables, benches etc. Twelve workers were found to possess a black and white television set.

The female bidi workers had to manage simultaneously their own household task. They had to combine wage work with their domestic responsibilities. It is found that in addition to bidi rolling, the workers had to do sundry work for their own family. The survey reveals that so far as the fuel collection and maintenance of house were concerned, the role of the husbands or other family members was noteworthy. The workers had nearly full responsibilities on the activities like washing clothes and utensils, water collection, food preparation and childcare. Apart from the large bulk of sundry task, often some workers had to help their husbands in agriculture activity.

The contribution of female bidi rollers to their families was in no way negligible. It is observed that in the economic sphere the status of most of the female bidi workers was similar as that of their husbands. 10.5 per cent of the workers could contribute more than Rs 600 per month to their family. Most of the workers contributed in the range of Rs. 301 to Rs. 500 per month (60.5 per cent). Among the child labourers, majority was found to spend a part of their earnings for the education.

It is found that 38.5 per cent of the workers had no savings potentialities in real sense. No worker was found to have saving account in post office or bank. 19.5 per cent of the workers saved certain amount of money at home, while 42 per cent of the workers were compelled to contribute provident fund at the rate of 10per cent of wage earned, where at the sometime employer also contributed at the rate of 11.67 per cent. However, only factory workers had to contribute to provident fund.

Table 3.6 reveals daily work profile of female bidi workers of different age group. The table is prepared

Table 3.6
Daily Work Profile of Bidi Workers

Time	*Child labour*	*Young age group group*	*Middle age group*
5.00 am	—	—	Rises
6.00 am	Rises	Rises	Taking breakfast does household task
7.00 am	Taking break-fast involves in study	Taking breakfast does household task	Feeding children rolls bidis
7.30 am	Engages in study	Roll bidis	Carries on rolling
9.00 am	Roll bidis	Carries on rolling	Prepares food for family
10.30 am	Taking food goes to school	Prepares food / Helps mother	Serving food rolls bidis
12.30 pm	Stays in school	Rolls bidis	Carries on rolling
3.00 pm	Returning home takes food and plays with friends	Takes food and rest	Takes food and rest
4.00 pm	Rolls bidis	Rolls bidis	Rolls bidis
5.00 pm	Carries on rolling	Interacts with family members	Interacts with neighbours
6.00 pm	Involves in study	Rolls bidis	Rolls bidis
8.00 pm	Engages in study	Prepares food / Helps mother	Prepares food
9.00 pm	Takes food	Serves food	Serving food interacts with children
9.30 pm	Goes to bed	Takes food	Takes food
10.00 pm	—	Goes to bed	Goes to bed

taking into consideration of average activities performed by the respondents. Column 2 shows activities of child labourers. The activities of a worker in the young age group are disclosed in column 3 and column 4 shows a day of a woman in the middle age group. The daily activities of the bidi workers have been stated as under:

SUMMARY

The economic significance of bidi industry as regard to gross value generation and foreign exchange earnings is not negligible. Besides, the industry absorbs a large number of female workers in India. Though the government has launched various welfare measures for the bidi workers by passing several legislations, still the workers have been facing acute problems like disparity in minimum wage and lack of social security.

The bidi workers are generally recruited by the principal employer or by the contractor. The employer supplies required raw materials to the workers who roll bidis at their own premises and deposit the finished product to the employer in a stipulated time. Sometimes, the workers have to purchase extra quantity of raw materials from outside to make good the deficit. The wages rate for bidi workers in West Bengal largely differs from one brand owner to another. However, direct factory workers get a lucrative wage than the contract labourers. They are provided other benefits like provident fund contribution and ex-gratia in addition to regular cash wages. The contract labourers are deeply exploited by paying a low wage.

The survey reveals that main concentration of female bidi workers is middle age group and existence of child labour in bidi rolling is also notable. The aged workers do not engage in bidi rolling because of their eyesight problems. Many workers are facing acute health crisis by the tobacco flakes and tendu leaves they handle.

The economic compulsion is the main reason of the workers behind taking the job as bidi rollers. However, many child labourers join the work force for meeting their educational expenses. The educational attainment of the female bidi workers is not sound except some school going child labour. The workers contribute a major part of their earnings to the family and few workers save money thinking for the future. Hence, female bidi workers are carrying out bidi rolling with their other domestic responsibilities in systematic way.

The female bidi workers are deprived of the minimum wages and the benefits of welfare provisions in the existing legislation. However, it is observed that female bidi workers in West Bengal have been joined the workforce mainly because of economic compulsion. They can never earn enough to become financially independent due to their minimum cash wages. With a view to improving the working conditions of female bidi workers the following suggestions are recommended.

First, imparting proper health education among the workers.

Secondly, providing minimum wages as fixed by the government.

Thirdly, providing standardized raw material and sufficient quantity not falling short of actual requirement by the employers.

Fourthly, implementing statutory social security schemes like Provident Fund and Insurance for all workers.

Fifthly, prohibiting rejection of bidis within normal limit.

Sixthly, imparting vocational education for child bidi labour.

Seventhly, minimizing gulf gap of wage rate between direct workers and contract workers.

Eighthly, making aware of different bidi welfare

schemes and location of health dispensaries at far-off places among the workers.

Ninthly, relaxing welfare provisions in the existing legislation for workers to avail full access to the benefits of schemes.

Lastly, encouraging saving potentialities amongst the workers.

REFERENCES

Avachat, A. (1978), *Beedi Workers of Nipani. Economic & Political Weekly*, XIII (30): 1203-1205.

Directorate of Tobacco Development (1990) *Non-Virginia Tobacco in India: A Status Paper.* Madras.

Giriappa, S. (1987), *Bidi Rolling in Rural Development.* Daya Publishing House, Delhi.

Government of India (1981), *Report on Working and Living Conditions of Workers in Bidi Industry.* Labour Bureau, Ministry of Labour.

Government of India (1994-95), *Report on Socio-Economic Conditions of Women Workers in Selected Beedi Units in India.* Ministry of Labour.

Government of India (1995), *Unorganised Sector Services: Report on the Working and Living Conditions of Workers in Beedi Industry in India.* Ministry of Labour, Chandigarh/ Simla.

Mishra, L. (2000), *Child Labourers in India.* Oxford University Press, New Delhi.

Mohandas, M. (1980), Beedi Workers in Kerala: Conditions of Life and Work. *Economic and Political Weekly*, Vol. XV, No. 36, pp. 1517-1523.

Mohandas, M. and Praveen Kumar, P.V. (1992), Impact of Co-operativisation on Working Conditions: Study of Beedi Industry in Kerala. *Economic and Political Weekly*, XXVII (26): 133-138.

Rajasekhar, D. and Sreedhar, G. (2002), Changing Face of Beedi Industry: A Study in Karnataka. *Economic and Political Weekly*, XXXVII (39): 4023-4028.

Saravanan, V. (2001), *A Report on the Linkages between Women's Employment and Reduction of Child Labour: The Case of Beedi Workers in Tamil Nadu.* ILO, Geneva.

Srinivasan, R. (1999), *Study on the Problems Faced by Beedi Rolling Workers.* Unpublished Project Report, Sacred Heart College, Tirupattur.

Tobacco Institute of India (1996) The Enemy within. *Tobacco News*, October.

Tobacco Institute of India (1997), Bounty of Tobacco: Some Glimpses. *Tobacco News*, January.

Tobacco Institute of India (1997), Beedi Workers–An Exploited Lot. *Tobacco News*, December.

Chapter - 4

Female Sex Workers

INTRODUCTION

The term sex work can be regarded as the practice of a group of human being either male or female, who involves in sexual relation with a different number of individuals having opposite or similar sex for some sort of monetary benefits or otherwise. But in reality, the term is used to denote female giving sexual pleasure and satisfaction to male folk in lieu of money. The sexual relations may be of various types, namely, sexual intercourse, verbal sex, masturbation, petting, deep kissing, telephone, and online sex. Therefore, precisely sex work can be defined as the act of a female who hires her body on a contractual basis to a number of males for sexual intercourse. Since informal sector is very diverse and it covers many types of work, the activities carried out by a sex worker fall under the category of 'own-account workers' in the informal sector. The sex workers do not work for an employer but have several customers of their own. They fix their own rate according to the type and quality of services they provided for and work for their own place and convenience.

In nearly all settings, female sex workers are stigmatised group of people (Jenkins 2000). In India, female sex workers are vulnerable high-risk group for the acquisition and transmission of sexually transmitted infection (STI) and human immunodeficiency virus (HIV). In most countries, female sex workers and their clients are at the hart of STI and HIV epidemics. Having multiple sexual partners and a high prevalence of STI (and in some countries, HIV), they form a core group that should be given priority while planning STI and HIV prevention interventions. About 4 million Indians are infected with HIV, second only to South Africa and estimated 80 per cent are the result of heterosexual transmission. Research exposed staggering misconceptions surrounding HIV transmission and risk assessment. One in every three men who visited a commercial sex worker was unaware that a healthy looking individual could carry HIV (Pasha 2003). Sex workers in India have a high risk of infection not just because of their large number of sex partners, but also because the high prevalence of other sexually transmitted diseases (STDs) among them which further enhance the risk of HIV transmission. Consequently several HIV-AIDS interventions in India have been targeted at the commercial sex industry (NACO 1999).

Most projects to prevent HIV/AIDS transmission have adopted health promotion strategies comprised of educational activities to inform sex workers and their clients about sexual health, combined with condom promotion and access activities and improved health services with a particular focus on the treatment of STIs (Evans 1999). Other studies have adopted community development strategies whereby deliberate efforts are made to achieve community participation in the design and implementation of the intervention, in the belief that empowering sex workers is the key to ensuring the long term success of reducing sex workers vulnerability to HIV and other STIs (NSWP 1997). Bhave *et al.* (1995) in a study of Mumbai sex workers present anecdotal evidence showing that the fear of a loss in income is one of the most important factors deterring sex workers from using condoms, even after they are made aware of HIV/AIDS and the role that condoms play in preventing it. Ahlburg and Jensen (1998) show that there is a total absence of econometric work on prostitution. The primary reason for this is the extreme difficulty in gathering reliable data on sex workers since the profession is practiced either illegally or on the fringes of legality.

However, the literature on current situation of sex workers in India is limited. The survey conducted by Ghosh and Das (1990) among female sex workers in eight red light areas of Calcutta reveals that a female sex worker entertained on the average 2.7 clients per day. It was estimated that the total annual income generated by the sex workers in Calcutta was about Rs.30 crore. About Rs.20 crore of the total amount generated by female sex workers were shared by pimps, brothel-home workers, matrons and others. Gilada (1995) in a study of Mumbai red-light area has found that each female sex worker entertained on the average four clients per day. They resided in crowded rooms and got their daily food filthy cafeterias and vendors. Laboratory tests disclosed that about 90 per cent of the female sex workers had one or more kinds of sexually transmitted diseases. It is also found that daughter of female sex workers very often became sex workers themselves, and sons often became primps. Jana (1995) has studied female sex workers in *Sonagachi* red light area of Calcutta. According to him, the average number of clients per female sex workers per day was 3.3. In a survey of female sex workers in GB Road red-light area of Delhi, Pillai (1982) finds that about 80 per cent of the female sex workers were initiated to their profession by their poverty ridden family members–majority by fathers and husbands, as it was customary to do so in their families. About one-half of them had to entertain on the average five to six clients a day. About three fourth of the female sex workers were suffering from sexually transmitted diseases at the time of survey.

SCOPE AND METHODOLOGY

The objectives of the study are to delve into the demographic characteristics, knowledge of HIV/AIDS, condom utilization and experience with STDs among female sex workers in Darjeeling hills of West Bengal .An attempt has also been made to classify the sex workers into different category. The data for the study were collected from a random sample of 128 female sex workers consisting of forty-two brothel based sex workers, sixty-five floating sex workers and twenty-one call girls. Several information on female sex workers had been gathered from extensive survey of field investigation and primary data collection was carried out by obtaining individual responses to the questionnaire. While survey instrument was primarily focused mainly on demographic characteristics, a number of socio-economic questions were also asked. Each potential respondent was given a brief explanation as to the purpose of study and they were assured that their response to the questionnaire would be anonymous.

CLASSIFICATION OF SEX WORKERS

The sex workers may be classified as under:

(a) *Brothel Complex-Based Female Sex Workers:* They have fixed place for entertaining their clients. They stay in the location, which is commonly known as red light area. In many cities, towns or villages there are a number of brothels, but it is difficult to identify them.

(b) *Floating Female Sex Workers*: They do not have any fixed place for meeting and entertaining their clients. This category of sex workers generally ramble streets,

public parks, railway stations, bus stands and areas surrounding cinema halls, hotels, restaurants etc.

(c) *Call Girls:* Call girls are part-time female sex workers who usually do not fulfill demand of their clients at own residents. They generally get clients via agents who contract with potential customers. The negotiations are generally carried out over telephone.

(d) *Transgender or Hijras:* The term transgender refers to a person, whose genitals are ambiguously male like at birth. A tiny percentages of those often called 'hijra' in India are physiologically hermaphrodite. Mostly they are castrated males. They gain their living by getting payment for their music and dance performance at homes on the occasion of male birth, wedding and other festivals.

(e) *Male Sex Workers:* Male sex workers provide sexual service to homosexually based men and heterosexually based women in lieu of cash or kind. A large chunk of young adults in India earn their livelihood by providing massage services to men in parks, sea beaches, hotels, saloons as well as homes. Many needy boys employed in small establishments are reported to be exploited by their male employers.

OBSERVATIONS OF STUDY

The major findings of the study were as follows:

(a) Socio-Economic and Demographic Characteristics

One hundred and fifty female sex workers were asked to participate in the study. Finally, one hundred and twenty eight of them agreed to complete the survey with a participation rate of eighty five per cent. The age of a sex worker is an attribute of her physical attractiveness. The main concentration of female sex workers was in the age group of 18 to 25 and the mean age of respondents was 20.6. The studies revealed that presence of aged female sex workers were comparatively low. At the same time, 3.2 per cent of the female sex workers were virtually girl child in the sense that they were in the age of below 14. Among floating sex workers and call girls, five were housewives and seven workers were students of either school or college. Further, the respondents were asked to indicate the age at which they took their first job. The mean age at first sex was found to be 16.2. It was further observed that the mean number of years as female sex workers was 6.6, with a range of 4 to 12 years.

The overall level of education of female sex workers was poor. The number of female sex workers who reported having completed middle or high school education appeared to be insignificant. Almost 12 per cent of the respondents reported that they completed middle or high school levels and 26 per cent of them had primary schooling experience. It was quite encouraging to find eight graduate female sex workers too. The remainder had no education at all. It was further observed that sex workers as floating and call girl tended to indicate better educational level compared to their counterparts in brothel complex.

Only 11 per cent of female sex workers were married and most of them had children with 0.6 children on average. The presence of maidens and divorced or separated female sex workers were relatively high. It was found that 57 per cent of the female sex workers were divorced and the number of widow female sex workers was only four.

Economic compulsion was the main reason behind taking the profession as sex workers. 35.2 per cent of the workers reported that they had chosen the profession for supporting either their father or husband. 61 per cent entered the profession in order to support themselves after being abandoned by their family member(s). There was no such worker in the findings who worked for mere sexual pleasure or passing out idle time. Five teen-aged workers were found who involved sex trade with a view to generating extra income. Most of the female sex workers argued that they are in extremely lucrative profession and this is why 7.8 per cent of the sex workers entered the occupation voluntarily. The average daily earnings of a female sex worker were in the tune of Rs.150 to Rs.250. They charged an average of Rs.50 to Rs.150 per act. However, the rate may vary according to the nature of services to be provided by the sex workers. The number of clients to be entertained a day by a female sex worker largely depends on a set of different characteristics, especially their physical attributes as well as type and quality of services they provide for. A female sex worker entertained a mean of 3 clients per day. An average sex worker generally gets one day off, serves an average 8.2 hours a day, this indicates an approximate hourly wage rate of Rs.28. It was also found that 38.3 per cent of the respondents contributed to their family every month and most of the female sex workers having children at the age of formal education spent a part of their earnings for child education. 67 per cent of the female sex workers were concerned about the potentially of savings. They saved a portion of their earnings either into post office or bank. Twenty-two such workers were identified who had been covered under life insurance schemes.

(b) Knowledge of HIV/AIDS

The level of knowledge of HIV/AIDS among female sex workers was also noteworthy. The more likely a sex worker is to become infected with HIV/AIDS, if she has unprotected sex with several partners. Interestingly, 43 per cent of the sex workers replied correctly at least two appropriate ways of HIV/AIDS prevention. About 57.8 per cent of the sex workers reported that HIV could be avoided by sticking to one partner, though this is not an option open to them in their profession. 62.5 per cent of the respondents addressed that HIV can be avoided by using condoms. Although, 68.8 per cent of the workers admitted that HIV/AIDS is an occupational worry, but one fourth of them reported that they have several times discussed HIV/AIDS with any one else.

(c) Condom Utilization

The effective means of preventing transmission of HIV/AIDS for those who have sexual relations with multiple partners is by consistently using condoms. 53.1 per cent of the sex workers used condom to avoid STDs and pregnancy. Regarding source of condom, 84.4 per cent indicated that they are to purchase condom out of own pocket and 15.6 per cent of the workers reported that condoms are supplied in the place of work. It was estimated that sex workers who relatively attractive and, consequently have a high demand for their services may also be more willing to buy safe sex by using condoms. It was observed that an average of 2.6 condoms are used by a sex worker per day, with a range of 1 to 4. Most of the sex workers admitted that they are afraid of getting infected by their clients and likewise agreed that condoms can prevent these transmissions. The sex workers indicated that about half of the time per act they request the clients to use condom and clients simply refuse to use it. It was interestingly noted that foreign clients possess more knowledge and willingness to use condoms, perhaps because of much awareness of the risk of HIV/AIDS.

(d) Experience with STDs

The knowledge of STDs among respondents was limited. Most workers (50.8 per cent) were able to indicate only one or two popular types of STDs, namely, HIV/AIDS and syphilis. Only 8.6 per cent of the sex workers acquainted about other types of STDs, such as gonorrhea, vaginal discharge, hepatitis, chlamydia etc. Among the respondents, 24.2 per cent stated that they have been suffering from an STD. Of these 66.7 per cent sought medical treatment. Those who sought treatment tend to go to private practitioners (22.6 per cent) or a health clinic (54.8 per cent). Among those sex workers who did not seek medical treatment, the majority decided to treat themselves. Those who went through self-treatment of their symptoms were mostly floating sex workers and call girls.

SUMMARY

It was observed that sex trade is a phenomenon of poor socio-economic status of a section of the society. There are a large number of women who have been forced to the profession owing to utter poverty. Many of them engaged the profession in order to supporting the family after their husbands lost jobs. With a view to empowering female sex workers in the shadow economy the following suggestions have been made.

Protecting human rights of sex workers by passing out appropriate legislations.

Treating sex workers in fully ethical manner so that they can recognise and express their felt needs.

Extending protective socio-economic security coverage to the sex workers.

Improving general awareness of working conditions to sex workers, raising parental awareness of loss of human capital associated with girl child sex workers.

Initiating compulsory formal schooling for the children of sex workers by various governments and non-governments organizations.

Strengthening proper understanding among sex workers, clients and pimps.

Helping them to understand the conditions prevailing to ensure long-run HIV/AIDS and other STDs prevention.

Monitoring a gradual approach to behavioural change with condoms use among sex workers for safer sex.

REFERENCES

Ahlburg, D.A. and Jensen, E.R. (1998), The Economic of Commercial Sex Industry and Its Implications for HIV/ AIDS Prevention Policies. In Martha Ainsworth *et al.* (eds.) *Confronting AIDS: Evidence from Developing World.* European Commission, Brussels.

Brave, G., Lindan, C.P., Hudes, E.S., Dessai, S., Wagle, U., Tripathi, S.P. and Mandal, J.S. (1995), Impact of An Intervention on HIV, Sexually Transmitted Diseases, and Condom Use Among Sex Workers in Bombay, India. *AIDS*, 9: S21-S30.

Evans, C. (1999), *An Introduction Review of the Rationale, Role and Evaluation of Community Development Approaches in Interventions to Reduce HIV Transmission in Sex Work.* Population Council, New Delhi.

Ghosh, M. and Das, N.K. (1990), *A Report on Prostitution in Calcutta.* Development Dialogue, Calcutta.

Gilada, I.S. (1995), *Women in Prostitution in Urban Centres: Study Perspectives and Prostitutional Problems for Social Interventions.* Unpublished Paper.

Jana, S. (1995), *Three Years Stint at Sonagachi: An Explosion.* Unpublished Paper.

Jenkins, C. (2000), *Female Sex Worker HIV Prevention Projects: Lesson Learnt from Papua New Guinea, India and Bangladesh.* UNAIDS, Geneva.

National AIDS Control Organization (NACO) (1999), *Country Scenario 1998-1999.* Ministry of Health and Family Welfare, New Delhi.

Network of Sex Worker Projects (NSWP) (1997), *Making Sex Work Safe.* Healthlink, London.

Pash, B. (2003), *HIV/AIDS Campaign Is the Talk of Mumbai*. Population Service International, Washington, D.C.

Pillai, V. (1982), Prostitution in India. *Indian Journal of Social Work*, 35 (4): 377-389.

Chapter - 5

Women Organizing for Social Security

INTRODUCTION

The protection that a society provides to individuals and households to ensure access to wage and working conditions in a comprehensive sense, in matters of security of employment, health care, maternity benefits, provident fund, retirement benefits, is an essential element of the safety nets that keeps working people and their families from falling into poverty. Social security is, however, a relative term. In the developing countries, it is used in a much broader sense than that used in the developed world (Ahmad *et al.* 1991; Ginneken 1998; Guhan 1994; Prabhu 2001a). It has been further recognised that the neglect of social opportunities due to lack of adequate progress in social security has been detrimental to economic and social development in the developing countries including India (Datta 1998: L-2). The informal sector, in particular, represents an important part of the economy and certainly of the labour market in many countries, especially developing countries, and poses a challenge to policy makers with regard to issues relating to improvement of the working condition and social protection of its workers. In India the informal sector employs over 90 per cent of the work force and 97 per cent of its women workers.. Most if not all, are not covered by meaningful social security schemes. The workforce in the informal sector is largely uneducated, possessing little or no skills. It suffers from social discrimination and as such is placed in a disadvantageous position. Workers who fall under the category of informal sector are drawn from the lower strata of the society, which further prevents their access to higher social and economic avenues. The informalised workforce is also unprotected labour.

Social security is both a concept as well as a structure. It represents basically a system of protection of individuals who are in need of such protection by the State as an agent of the society. Such protection is relevant in contingencies such as retirement, resignation, retrenchment, death and disablement that are beyond the control of the individual members of the society. State as a representative of the society has an important mandate to keep parity with such differences through a protective cover to the poor, the deprived and the disadvantaged. The concept of social security is now generally understood as meaning protection provided by the society to its members through a series of public measures against the economic and social distress that otherwise is caused by the stoppage or substantial reduction of earnings resulting from sickness, maternity, employment injury, occupational diseases, unemployment, invalidity, old age and death. The ILO concept of social security is based on the recognition of the fundamental social right guaranteed by law to all human beings who live from their own labour and who find themselves unable to work temporarily or permanently for reasons beyond their control. At the international level, the preamble of the charter of ILO also referred to the need and protection of workers against sickness, disease and injury arising out of their employment, pension for old age, protection of the interests of the workers who were employed in countries other than their own. Thus the right to social security was recognised officially for the first time. Social security has been recognised as an instrument for social transformation and progress and must be preserved, supported and developed as such. Furthermore, far from being an obstacle to economic progress as is often alleged, social security organised on a firm and sound basis will promote progress, since once men and women benefit from increased security and are free from anxiety will become more productive. There is considerable controversy about the social and economic effects of social security and most of the current debate is focused on its supposedly negative effects. Social security is supposed to discourage people from working and saving to reduce international competitiveness and employment creation and to encourage people to pull out from the labour market prematurely. On the other hand, social security can also be observed to have a number of very positive economic effects. It can help to make people capable of earning an income and to increase their productive potential, it may help to maintain effective demand at the national level and it may help create conditions in which a market economy can flourish, notably by encouraging workers to accept innovation and change. A formal social security system presupposes the interventionist role of the State on redistribution grounds. Social security measures are generally income, maintenance measures intended to provide a minimum living to the people when they are deprived of the same due to invalidity, unemployment or old age. The two basic elements of social security are provision of a minimum living to those who are deprived of the same and selective redistribution of income to a target group to reduce inequalities. Social security to the workers would involve providing or framing such schemes or services or facilities and amenities, which can enable the workers to lead a decent minimum standard of life and having economic security to fall back upon in the event of loosing job for whatsoever may be the reason in the circumstances beyond their control. The workers must be given the wages and other services, which will enable them and the members of their family to lead a decent life. Thus social security is an instrument for social transformation and good governance. Social security in India was traditionally the responsibility of the community in general. Currently ongoing measures towards transformation process has added a new dimension to the issue and enhanced the requirement further towards a planned and regulated institutionalised measure in the form of social security in its common understanding. Low-income women workers constitute one of the most vulnerable groups in Indian society. Their vulnerability arises from their irregular work, their low economic status, their little bargaining power, their lack of control over their earnings, their need to balance work with care for children and homework and their lack of assets. Unequal gender relations indeed assume an important role in defining their insecurities (Dasgupta 2003: 39).

CONCEPT

The concept of social security has been changing with the passage of time from traditional ways to modern forms of protection. While the definition of social security has been made comprehensive, however little attention has been paid to the working poor in the informal sector. It still eludes most workers in the informal sector, especially women workers (Jhabvala *et al*. 2002: 2041).

The ILO first proposed a comprehensive definition of social security as the protection measures which society provides for its members, through a series of public measures against economic and social distress that would otherwise be caused by the stoppages or substantial reduction of earnings resulting from sickness, maternity, employment injury, unemployment, disability, old-age death, provision of medical care and subsidies for families with children (ILO 1989). Most annotators agree that ILO definition is inadequate for developing countries (Subrahmanya 1994) and the components of social security listed in the definition are based on the experiences of developed countries. It is true that most people work, but their work is intermittent, insecure, and yields too little to cover the costs of social security. Moreover, often many of the components of social security are just not available to the workers at affordable prices (Jhabvala *et al.* 1998: L-8)

A good number of alternative definitions have been put forth to overcome the lacunae of the ILO definition. Subrahmanya (1994) defined social security as a guarantee by the whole community to all its members, of the maintenance of their standard of living, or at least of tolerable living conditions, by means of redistribution of income, based on national solidarity. In other words, the concept of social security in its broadest sense should be understood to mean the support provided to the individual by the society to enable him/her to attain a reasonable standard of living, and to protect him or her from falling due to the occurrence of any contingency.

Getubig (1992) proposed a definition which is based on the expansion of the elements of social security to include any kind of collective measures or activities designed to ensure that member of society meet their basic needs (such as adequate nutrition, shelter, health care and clean water supply) and are protected from contingencies (such as illness, disability, death, unemployment and old-age) so that they are enabled to maintain a standard of living consistent with social norms. Hence, the definition of social security is extended to include of other aspects of existence, which relate to accessing adequate food, health care and shelter to vulnerable groups.

The concept of social security, therefore, implies a broad pro-poor approach which has three major components namely, a promotional component that aims at improving endowments, exchange entitlements, real incomes and social consumption, a preventive component that seeks to avert deprivation in more specific ways and a protective component (also known as safety measures) that is yet more specific in generating relief against deprivation (Hirway 1995).

According to Guhan (1994), social protection in poor countries has to be viewed as part or fully integrated with anti-poverty polices, with such polices themselves being broadly conceived in view of the complex, multi-dimensional nature of poverty and deprivation.

A broader connotation of social security is enunciated by Dreze and Sen (1989) essentially as an objective pursued through public means rather than as a narrowly set of particular strategies. The wider connotation of social security has also been termed as socio-economic security since it comprises measures that aim at improving social capabilities and enhances average income level of the general population (Prabhu 2001 b).

The narrower definitions of social security presume that members of society have already achieved a satisfactory standard of living and the major objective of social security is to protect individuals from a fall in this standard of living. Moreover, it is assumed that majorities of the people have access to regular work, and thereby income, and those only specific contingencies need to be handled through public policy (Mahendra Dev *et al.* 2001). These definitions have been extremely useful in drawing a different dimension of social security in developing countries. The problem, however, is that in so broadening the scope, the emphasis is on programmes of employment, income and poverty alleviation which are immense, complex, politically sensitive and have taken up considerable resources and attention of governments, non-government organizations, trade unions, political parities and in fact of all groups concerned with development and/ or social justice (Jhabvala *et al.* 1998: L-8).

Socio-economic security is a wider notion than social security. The term socio-economic security is more comprehensive and it refers to the security of not only having remunerative work, but also having possibilities of advancement in one's career, as well as access to benefits and control over one's work. It is defined that socio-economic security differs from social security in not being only possibility based, but also work based. Work-based socio-economic securities have been defined by Standing (1999) to include labour market security (opportunities for productive employment in the labour market), employment security (protection against employment loss), work security (protection against accidents and illness at work), skill reproduction security (widespread opportunities to gain and retain skills, through apprenticeships, employment training, etc.), income security (protection of adequate and regular income) and representation security (the protection of a collective voice in the labour market). In addition to these, security of other aspects of existence that relate to accessing adequate food, health care and shelter can be comprehended as basic security. Basic security is therefore security of access to basic amenities and opportunities. leave, and women vendors, for example, face harassment from public authorities. The workers in informal sector also lack basic security. This is because in a situation of low work-based socio-economic security, in the absence of social infrastructure or a social protection system that guarantees each person decent basic amenities, basic security remains low (Dasgupta 2003:44).

EXISTING MODEL

Social security comprises of two types of measures namely, promotional and protective. Promotional measures consist mainly of employment, training and nutrition schemes by which a person is able to work and earn a livelihood. Protective measures consist of schemes by which the State provides the means of livelihood when a person is not able to work (Subrahmanya 2000). ILO standards relating social security are mainly protective and have been designed primarily for the formal sector. There are many possible measures for social security provision for the informal sector, but two specific models have been explored as follows.

(a) *Welfare Funds:* Welfare funds represents one of the methods for providing social security to the workers in the informal sector in India. Welfare funds are of two types, namely, contributory and tax based. The funds set up by the central government are tax based, while those set up by the government of Kerala are mostly contributory. A contributory scheme is akin to social insurance. In India, there is only one social insurance scheme, namely, the employees' social insurance scheme. The funds may be administered departmentally or by autonomous body and are financed by the central as well as State governments. The other scheme, namely, the government of India's, tax based welfare funds cover mine workers, beedi rollers, cine workers and workers in building and construction industry. The fund is administered by the office of the director general, labour welfare, through its regional offices and financed by special levies in the forms of cess.

The State funds are mainly contributory based on contributions from employers, workers and government, and administered by labour departments of respective State governments. The funds cover wide range of facilities including health care, education for children, housing and water supply, old-age and survivor benefits, group insurance schemes and recreational facilities. The central welfare funds for mine workers and beedi rollers may be used for improvement of public health and sanitation, prevention of disease, and provision and improvement of medical facilities, water supplies and facilities for washing, educational facilities, standards of living including housing and nutrition, amelioration of social conditions and provision of recreational facilities, family welfare including family planning and other services. Although the model has been implementing successfully in India, still, mine and beedi workers have no provision for meeting the expenditure on any of the well recognised branches of social security like benefits of sickness, occupational injury, maternity, invalidity, old-age, survivor or unemployment.

(b) *Insurance Corporations*: Insurance corporations in India have been providing social insurance to the workers in the informal sector. With the assistance of Central and State governments, they have introduced various schemes, which are administered directly through government or more successfully through cooperatives and non-government organizations and are a combination of social assistance and social insurance. The Life Insurance Corporation (LIC) in India has developed group insurance, which is akin to social insurance based on large numbers. It has the potential to provide social security to those in the informal sector. The scheme

offers life insurance cover at a premium of Rs. 10 for every Rs. 10,000 of benefits. Up to Rs. 5,000 coverage is subsidised up to 50 per cent by one time capital grant from the government. This model has been adopted by the central government, State governments and voluntary organizations to cover the life insurance of many groups of workers in the informal sector. The largest of these schemes, where the premium is contributed by the central government, is for landless agricultural workers. There are many other group insurance schemes for workers in the informal sector, for milk producers, handloom weavers, rickshaw pullers, shop assistants, sweepers, beedi workers, fish farmers and others. The scheme of the LIC provide mainly survivor benefits, some also provide old-age pensions too. Apart from the LIC, the General Insurance Corporation (GIC) of India also administers a few social security schemes such as personal accident social security scheme for poor families, the hut insurance scheme and the solatium fund. The GIC has also launched a health insurance scheme and has been monitoring the comprehensive group insurance scheme for the central government. The schemes of the GIC include invalidity benefits, health insurance and protection against loss of property.

Some other schemes of social security protection in the informal sector include:

- Childcare services to workingwomen, especially creches for children of working mothers have been implemented by the Central Social Welfare Board.
- Under National Maternity Benefit Scheme, central assistance is provided in the form of payment of Rs.300 each to pregnant women for first two childbirths.

- Under Family Benefit Scheme, central assistance is given in the form of payment of a lump sum of Rs.5000 to families below the poverty line on the death of their breadwinner.
- Under National Old-age Pension Scheme, central assistance is extended to States for payment of old-age pension to men and women who have attained the age of 65 or more at Rs. 75 per month.
- Assistance in case of sickness, either in the form of a lump sum or reimbursement of medical expenses, assistance in case of death of bread winner and maternity assistance is provided by many voluntary organizations as well as co-operative societies.

INITIATIVES

Several State governments of India have taken initiatives to provide various protective social security measures for workers in the informal sector. A few States such as Andhra Pradesh, Gujarat, Kerala and Tamil Nadu also have special pension schemes for agricultural workers. Maternity benefits for landless agricultural labour have been introduced in Gujarat, Karnataka and Kerala to compensate loss of wage due to absence at work. However, health care as a part of the social security does not seem to exist in any State. Gujarat, Tamil Nadu and Kerala have certain welfare schemes exclusively for women and children while a number of other States offer welfare benefits for various categories of population below the poverty line.

Successive governments in Kerala have introduced a number of social security and welfare schemes in view of attaining the goal of minimizing income insecurity among the weaker sections. It has various schemes for the benefits of the informal sector (Rajan *et al.* 1999). The most important protective type schemes in terms of coverage are old-age pensions for destitute and rural labourers. Another innovative programme in Kerala is the creation of welfare funds. In order to meet the demands of the informal sector workers, some types of social insurance and other non-wage benefits, a new institutional innovation was come into limelight in the form of welfare funds. With the active support from the trade unions, the government of Kerala took the initiative to create a fund through contributions from worker, employers and government.

Apart from the Kerala, Tamil Nadu has been a pioneer in implementing social security protection for the workers in the informal sector (Guhan 1993). The main initiatives are liberalized pensions, accident relief scheme, new survivor benefit scheme, maternity assistance scheme and marriage grant scheme. It has been implementing protective social security for providing nutrition to vulnerable groups such as pregnant and destitute women and the aged and the like. Other States in India and developing countries can learn from the experiences of Kerala and Tamil Nadu on what can be done in the area of protective social security measures at reasonable cost to help the vulnerable groups. Some other States have also taken important initiatives in recent years, namely, employment guarantee scheme in Maharashtra, primary education in Himachal Pradesh and Madhya Pradesh, public distribution in Andhra Pradesh and land reform in West Bengal. In contrast, in States like Bihar, Uttar Pradesh, Rajasthan, there seems to be apathetic towards the necessity to build social security schemes (Mahendra Dev 2000).

A number of State governments have also set up welfare funds for various categories of workers. The government of Kerala has set up about 35 welfare funds for different categories of occupations and sectors. These welfare funds cater to the needs of agricultural workers, auto rickshaw workers, cashew workers, coir workers, construction workers, fishermen and women, handloom workers etc.

The government of Assam has set up a statutory fund under Assam Plantation Employees Welfare Fund Act, 1959 for the benefit of the plantation workers. Similar funds have also been set up in Gujarat and Maharashtra under Bombay Labour Welfare Fund Act, 1953 and in Karnạtaka under Mysore (Karnataka) Labour Welfare Act, 1965 and in Punjab under the Labour Welfare Act, 1965.

The State governments of Andhra Pradesh and Uttar Pradesh have also set up welfare funds for various categories of workers. All these welfare funds however, cater to a very small segment of the total workforce. In view of the change in the perception of the social security i.e., an essential input to the productivity rather than burden on exchequer, some State governments are making concerted efforts to extend social security to the workers in the informal sector. For instance, the government of Karnataka is going to set up a social security authority of Karnataka and create a welfare board to cater to the needs of the 66 identified occupational groups shortly. Further, occupational groups can be added to it as and when the necessity arises. The welfare fund will be created by levying a cess from transport vehicles, employer's contribution, workers and the State government when there is no employer. The fund created therein will be utilised to implement schemes and programmes covering pension, health, housing, insurance in case of death and disability aspects for the benefit of workers.

Recently, the government of West Bengal initiated State Assisted Scheme of Provident Fund for Unorganised Workers. The scheme covers all wage employed and self-employed workers between the ages of 18 to 55 years in the unorganised sector having an average family income of not more than Rs. 3500 per month. Each subscriber worker contributes a sum of Rs.20 per month and equal matching amount contributed by the state government. The interest on the balance at credit of subscriber is also paid by the state government annually at the rate declared by the State government. Total contribution along with interest has to be refunded to the worker on attainment of the age of 55 years. The scheme will have provision for loans and withdrawals from the fund as prescribed by the State government. The government of West Bengal had identified 50 industries in the unorganised sector and 16 self-employed occupations, of which 13 unorganised industries and 7 self-employed occupations are being covered in the first phase. These industries include tailoring shops, establishments having less than 20 workers, bakery, handloom, construction, earthen pottery, stone crushing, auto repairing, etc. The self-employed occupations include cycle rickshaw, head load workers, railway/street hawkers, auto rickshaw operators, mason and cobblers.

The Department of Agriculture of the State of Punjab implements a scheme financed from the funds available with marketing committees/boards to provide financial assistance to the farmers and labourers in case of death or injury by operating the agricultural machinery/ implements and undertaking other operations both at the level of farm since 1984. The scope of the scheme includes death or disablement to any farmer or labour working in the agricultural machinery implements or arising out of the use of the said machinery implements in the state of Punjab, death or disablement to any farmer or labour arising out of digging of tube-well in the State of Punjab or electric current while operating tube-well in the farm, death or disablement to any farmer or labour while using the insecticides or pesticides in the State of Punjab or due to snake biting while working in field or watering the field and death or disablement to labour employed in field arising out of use of agricultural machinery implements. The financial assistance provided under the scheme includes payment of Rs. 75,000 in case of death, Rs. 30,000 in case of partial disability such as loss of one leg, eye, arm or serious injury, Rs. 45,000 in case a farmer or labour lost both eyes, arms, leg, etc. Rs. 7,500 to Rs. 22,500 in case of loss of fingers and Rs. 30,000 in case of loss of four fingers, which is treated as loss of one arm. The group was apprised of the free medical check up camps being organised by the government of Punjab. Workers working in hazardous and dangerous process establishments come in contact with various toxic substances and other chemicals from which they are likely to contact with occupational diseases. The government of Punjab has decided to carry out free medical check up of such workers. Till date 165 medical check up camps have been organised in which 50,000 workers have been examined and medicines worth Rs. 18 lakhs were spent in these camps by the employers which generated a lot of goodwill. 3500 workers were referred to hospitals for their blood test, chest X-rays, surgical operations, skin diseases, leprosy etc. This is a very welcome step in the right direction as it demonstrates the willingness of the State to share the burden in delivery of health services.

The government of Tamil Nadu introduced Tamil Nadu Social Security and Welfare Scheme-2001. These schemes cover manual worker, auto rickshaws and taxi drivers, washer-men, hairdressers, tailoring workers, handicraft workers and palm tree workers. The State government is planning to formulate scheme for handlooms and handloom silk-weaving workers, footwear and leather goods manufacturing and tannery workers and artists. State government has set up the goal and social security and welfare fund for the respective workers. Every worker registered under the scheme for two years initially has to pay a sum of Rs. 100 and every employer 3 per cent of the wages payable by him to the worker employed to the social security and welfare board. The fee for renewing the registration is Rs. 10. The funds are to be utilized for paying premium towards insurance coverage having provision of compensation of Rs. 1 lakh in case of death or loss of both hands, feet, Rs. 50,000 in case of loss of one hand or one foot and Rs. 25,000 in case of permanent total disablement from injuries other than loss of limbs or death. The financial assistance is extended to the tune of Rs. 10,000 to the nominee of the deceased worker in case of natural death and Rs. 2,000 to meet the funeral expenses. Assistance of Rs. 1,000 for the education of the son or daughters of the workers passing 10th Standard examination, Rs. 1500 for passing plus two examination and studying in regular bachelor degree course and Rs. 2,000 in case of post graduate course or professional course for every academic year is provided through the fund. A sum of Rs. 2,000 is extended to the applicant or his son or daughter for marriage. Further, assistance is also extended for delivery or the miscarriage or pregnancy or the termination of pregnancy by a registered female worker to the extent of Rs. 2,000.

In addition to governmental efforts, several public institutions and agencies are also providing various kinds of social security benefits to selected groups of workers. Two of the outstanding examples are those of Self-Employed Women's Association (SEWA) and the Mathadi Workers Boards in Maharashtra. The social security experiments of SEWA started in 1975 with a demand from members for a maternal protection scheme followed by health care and childcare. This was followed by starting of an insurance programme in collaboration with insurance companies. The insurance scheme started by the SEWA Bank was based on a realistic estimate of the capacity of the members to pay the premium. An Integrated Insurance Scheme introduced by SEWA for its members, offers several benefits for a consolidated annual premium of Rs. 45. While SEWA itself provides some of the benefits, it works as a nodal agency to get cover under various policies separately for specific benefits from different insurance companies. The risk covered includes health costs upto Rs. 1,000, maternity benefit of Rs. 300 and payment of varying amounts upto Rs. 10,000 in case of natural or accidental death including disablement of the member or her husband. The insurance scheme has turned out to be both popular and financially viable. The total coverage of SEWA social security scheme is about 50,000 women. The experience of SEWA reveals that in order to become effective, the social security scheme for the informal sector should be locally managed and controlled. Further, only such schemes will become viable which are need based and integrated with the economic activities of the local people. If poor people are supported through capacity building and necessary linkages are provided with their own economic activities the chances of success of social security efforts increased significantly. Further, it has demonstrated that, it is not only necessary to search new social security programmes but new social security organizations to run them.

A *mathadi* is a worker who carries a load on his head, back, neck or shoulders. Normally his work consists of loading, unloading, carrying, shifting, weighing, tapping, banding and stacking goods. In the State of Maharashtra, the Mathadi Labour Market is regulated by Mathadi Tripartite Boards set up since 1969. There are about 50,000 registered employers and 1,50,000 workers registered under 30 different boards in the State. The Mathadi Workers Boards, besides settling disputes between unions and employers, are actively involved in imparting social security benefits to their members by setting up of hospitals and dispensaries. At present there are two hospitals with an annual budget of Rs.2 crores which are run by six Mathadi Boards. In addition to this, there are 12 dispensaries. Each of the six Boards contributes 2 per cent of their levy and each worker contributes Rs. 20 per month. These hospitals provide diagnostic services such as radiology, pathology and sonography for around 40,000 workers and their families. During the last few years, some of the Mathadi Boards have been able to get the workers registered with them insured against accident, injuries and death. For example, Mathadi Boards in Pune are paying Rs. 152 per annum as premium out of the Board's administrative account to cover workers for a benefit of Rs. 25,000 in case of injury and Rs. 2,00,000 in case of death to each worker. This scheme has been worked out by the Mathadi Board with the General Insurance Corporation. Besides organizations like Co-operative Development Foundation (CDF), Trivandrum District Fishermen Federation (TDFF), the Association of Sarwa Sewa Farms (ASSF), the Society for Promotion of Area Resources Centre (SPARC), Voluntary Health Services (VHS) in Tamil Nadu and the Working Women's Forum have experimented for providing social security to small groups of people. The VHS in Chennai and the Association for Health Welfare in Nilgiris (ASHWINI) in the tribal areas of Gudalur in Tamil Nadu have made efforts to provide medical care to very specific target groups. The approach of these agencies is based on collecting of contribution from the beneficiaries themselves for their future contingencies in line with the insurance principles.

CHALLENGES

Efforts to extend social security coverage to the informal sector face a number of challenges:

- Inadequate social security expenditure as well as inefficient utilization of funds under government and non-government programmes.

- Higher transaction costs due to the additional costs arising out enforcing compliance to extend social security coverage to the informal sector in urban and rural areas.
- Non-existence of loan facilities and sponsorship for training to the workers in informal sector in the conventional social security protection schemes.
- Lack of contribution capability due to low income to the existing insurance schemes for their future protection.
- Lack of support from the workers to some non-statutory welfare funds having negligible benefits.

SUMMARY

There is an urgent need to provide social security to the workers in the informal sector. The social security measures should cover provision of insurance, social security funds and childcare. It is also essential to supplement minimum wages by social security measures for the utmost social and economic benefits to the workers in the informal sector.

With a view to extending social security protection to the informal sector in India the following recommendations are made:

- Strengthening member organization based as well as community and private household based systems for comprehensive social security protection.
- Encouraging State governments in formulating and implementing schemes for certain occupations in the informal sector without creating too much pressure on budgetary allocation.
- Launching awareness campaigns on minimum wages in collaboration with voluntary organizations.
- Setting up co-operatives, self-help groups and mutual

benefits associations managed and financed by the occupation groups.

- Initiating welfare funds model by all the State governments for certain categories of workers in the informal sector.

REFERENCES

Ahmad, E., Dreze, J. and Sen, A. (eds.) (1991), Social Security in Developing Countries. Clarendon Press, Oxford.

Dasgupta, S. (2003), Women Organizing for Socio-Economic Security. *The Indian Journal of Labour Economics*, 46 (1): 39-68.

Datta, R.C. (1998), Public Action, Social Security and Unorganised Sector. *Economic and Political Weekly*, XXXIII (22): L2-L5.

Dreze,J. and Sen, A. (1989), *Hunger and Public Action*. Clarendon Press, Oxford.

Getubig, I.P. and Schmidt, S. (1992), *Rethinking Social Security: Reaching out to Poor*. Asian and Pacific Development Centre, Kula Lumpur.

Ginneken, W.V. (1998), *Social Security for all Indians*. Oxford University Press, New Delhi.

Guhan, S. (1993) Social Security for the Poor in the Unorganised Sector: A Feasible Blueprint for India. In K.S. Parikh *et al.* (eds.) *Human Development and Structural Adjustment*. Macmillan, Madras.

Guhan, S. (1994), Social Security Options for Developing Countries. *International Labour Review*, 133 (1): 35-53.

Hirway, I. (1995), *Social Security for the Rural Poor in the Context of Structural Adjustment*. Unpublished Paper.

International Labour Organization (1989) *Introduction to Social Security*. Geneva.

Jhabvala, R. (1998), Social Security for Unorganised Sector. *Economic and Political Weekly*, XXXIII (22): L7-L11.

Jhabvala, R. (2002), Liberalization and the Women Workers. *Economic and Political Weekly*, XXXVII (22): 2037-2044.

Mahendra Dev, S. (2000), *Growth-Mediated and Support-Led Social Security in the Unorganised Sector in India*. Invest India Economic Foundation.

Mahendra Dev, S., Antony, P., Gayathri,V. and Mamgani,R.P. (2001), *Social and Economic Security in India*. Institute for Human Development, New Delhi.

Prabhu, K.S. (2001a), *Economic Reforms and Social Development*. Sage Publications, New Delhi.

Prabhu, K.S. (2001b), *Socio-Economic Security in the Context of Pervasive Poverty: A Case Study of India*. SES Papers No. 9, International Labour Organization, Geneva.

Rajan, I., Mishra, U.S. and Sarma, P.S. 1999. *India's Elderly: Burden or Challenge*. Sage Publications, New Delhi.

Standing, G. (1999), *Global Labour Flexibility: Seeking Social Justice*. McMillan Press. London.

Subrahmanya, R.K.A. (1994) *Social Security in Developing Countries*. Har Anand Publication, New Delhi.

Subrahmanya, R.K.A. (2000), Support for the Unorganised Sector: Existing Social Security Measures. In: R. Jhabvala *et al.* (eds.). *The Unorganised Sector: Work Security and Social Protection*. Sage Publications, New Delhi.

Chapter - 6

Existing Health Insurance for Poor

INTRODUCTION

In India the informal sector employs more than 90 per cent of workforce, most if not all, are covered by meaningful social security schemes. The term social security in developing countries is used in much broader sense than that used in developed countries (Ahmad *et al.* 1991, Guhan 1994, Prabhu 2001). It has been further recognised that the neglect of social opportunities due to lack of adequate progress in social security has been detrimental to the economic and social development in the developing countries including India (Datta 1998:L-2). The informalised workforce is unprotected labour, which imply labour that does not have any socio-economic safety. The protection that a society provides to individuals and households to ensure access to wage and working conditions in a comprehensive sense, in matters of security of émployment, health care, maternity benefits, provident fund, retirement benefits, is an essential element of the safety nets that keeps working people and their families from falling into poverty (Sarkar 2004 a: 122).

The informal sector represents an important part of the economy and certainly of labour market in many countries, especially developing countries and poses a challenge to policy makers with regard to issues relating to improvement of the working condition and social protection of the workers engaged in the informal sector. In the developing economies a substantial share of employment is indeed in informal category and women in all age groups depend on the informal sector more heavily than men. Women are over represented in this sector in the sense that their share in the sector is higher than their share in total labour force. Most women tend to be own account workers and only a few are heads of micro enterprises. Relatively lower level of education among women, compared to men, seems to explain, in part, this gender differential in informal employment. Discrimination in the labour market also explains in part the disproportionate concentration as it limits women's access to formal and wage employment. Women also face additional constraints because of their homemaking and childcare responsibilities, which limits their participation in formal employment. Even within the informal sector more women than men seem to be in poor quality employment. The causes for participation in the informal sector can be economic and non-economic. Economic reasons are related to unemployment and an inflexible formal labour market, a declining real price of capital and the high cost of formal production. Besides, non-economic causes are concerned with a greater flexibility and satisfaction in work, a complete use of workers professional qualifications and increased leisure time. There are two groups of factors, which determine the decision to become active in the informal sector, more specifically, the structural as well as opportunity factors. The structural factors consist of economic pressure, socio-psychological pressure and institutional constraints. The opportunity factors consist of individual background, skills, education, living condition or non-individual components, environment, values, standards etc. (Sarkar 2004 b: 366).

The realization that mere existence of health care facilities does not necessarily mean that they are readily accessible to the poorest section in the informal economy, tend to the evolution of a unique health insurance scheme, with contribution according to individual capacity. Health insurance protects against the cost of illness, mobilizes funds for health services, enhances the efficiency of mobilization of funds and provision of health services, and achieves certain equity objectives by continuously benchmarking. Previously insurance was not considered as an option for the poor in informal sector. They were regarded to be too poor to save and pay premium. It is being gradually recognised that even low-income group can make tiny contribution to health insurance schemes. Health insurance for the poor can take different forms namely, community based or non-community based insurance policy of the government. In recent years community health insurance has gained as a possible means of improving access to health care among the poor and protecting the poor from indebtedness and hardship resulting from medical expenditures. Non-governmental organizations (NGOs) play an important role in the delivery of affordable health services to the poor but their coverage has always remained diminutive (Table 6.1 and 6.2).

EXISTING SCHEMES

The various health care programmes are presently operating for the informal sector in developing countries. In India community and self-financing schemes, and micro-credit linked health insurance schemes are the important intermediate steps in the evolution of an

Table 6.1
Salient Characteristics of Select NGO Managed Health Insurance Schemes

Voluntary organizations / Location	*Date started*	*Service provided*	*Health service Delivery / Organisation*	*Population served*	*Total annual cost (Rs.)*
Sevagram/ Wardha, Maharasthra	Hospital, 1945 Community health programme 1972	1. 500 bed hospital 2. Out reach community health programme	– Trained male VHW provides basic curative, preventive and promotive health care. Mobile with doctor and ANM provides care every 2 months	– -19,457	-69,459
Bombay Mother and Child Welfare Society (BMCWS)/ Chawl in Bombay	1947	Health activities, Two maternity hospitals (40 beds each) with child welfare centres, Non-health activities, Day care centres, convalescent home	• Outpatient and inpatient maternity care • Outpatient pediatric care including immunization		120175 (health and non health combined)
Raigarh Ambikapur Health Association (RAHA)/	1969 Community health services started 1974	Federation of 3 referral hospitals and 65 independent health centres with outreach	• RAHA functions include management of insurance scheme, training and support for health centres.	400,000	30,000-50,000 (cost range of individual health centres of which

Contd....

Voluntary organizations / Location	*Date started*	*Service provided*	*Health service Delivery / Organisation*	*Population served*	*Total annual cost (Rs.)*
Raigarh, Madhya Pradesh		community care	• Health centres staffed by nurse provide outpatient care run MCH clinic • VHWs provide communitybased care		there are 65)
Christian Hospital/ Bissamaucuttak, Orissa	Hospital 1954, out reach community care 1980	120 bed hospital, community project currently not operational	Outpatient/inpatient care, specialties include obstetrics, gynecology, surgery, ophthalmology	–	1,911,740 (hospital only)
UPASI Coonoor, Tamil Nadu	19th century CLWS - 1971	Association of tea growers run comprehensive labour welfare scheme (CLWS)	CLWS provides training, management support to health programmes of individual tea estates. Tea estates have small cottage hospital and outreach care provided by local workers	250,000	300,000
Goalpur Co-operative Health Society/ Shantiniketan, West Bengal	1964	Dispensary, periodic community health services	Doctor provides outpatient care twice weekly	1,247	32,000

Contd....

Voluntary organizations / Location	Date started	Service provided	Health service Delivery / Organisation	Population served	Total annual cost (Rs.)
Students health home/ West Bengal	1955	Polyclinic plus 28 regional clinics	Polyclinic has 20 beds provides outpatient and inpatient care; Regional clinics, outpatient care only, health education campaigns, blood donation camps	550,000	2,950,745
Saheed Shabsankar Saba Samithi (SSSS)/ Burdwan, West Bengal	1978	Dispensary occupational health activities, rural health programme, school health programme, fair price medicine shop	Doctors provide outpatient care weekly MCH clinic	–	87,780
Arvind eye hospital/ Madurai, Tamil Nadu	1976	2 urban hospitals (100 beds), 2 rural hospitals (500 beds), outreach programme	Outpatient and inpatient eye care Regular eye camps organized	–	10,987,700
Tribovandas Foundation/ Anand, Gujarat	1980	Community based health programme linked with milk cooperatives, regional rehabilitation centres,	Community health workers (CHWs) Ws provide basic curative, preventive, and promotive care; field, supervisors	300,000	1,080,000 (health and non-health combined)

Contd.....

Voluntary organizations / Location	*Date started*	*Service provided*	*Health service Delivery / Organisation*	*Population served*	*Total annual cost (Rs.)*
		Balwadis women's income generating scheme	provide support to CHWs milk society building used as base for coordinating health services.		
SEWA/ Ahmedabad, Gujarat	Union 1972, health programme 1984	Union of self-employed women. Helps organize women into cooperatives of various traders, provides credit facilities. Provides health care as a support, which stocks rational generic drugs.	Health centres in urban slums and rural villages. CHWs provide basic care, doctors provide support twice weekly.	63,000	391,850 (health programme only)
CINI/ Daulatpur, West Bengal	1975	Community based health programmes, dispensary and out-reach rehabilitation centre. Other activities: income generating schemes, farm, health training, research	CHWs provide MCH care through Mahila Mandals, doctors run daily OPD, weekly MCH clinic, supplementary feeding	70,000 (Ccmmunity health project)	1,900,000

Source: Dave [1991].

Table 6.2
Prepayment and Insurance Mechanisms in Select NGO Managed Health Insurance Schemes

Features	*Sevagram*	*RAHA*	*Tribovandas Foundation*	*Goalpara*	*Students Health Home*	*SSSS*
Coverage provided	Household	Individual	Household	Household	Institutional and individual	Individual
Annual subscription fee	8 payali sorgham (Landless) and 2 payali sorgham per acre extra (land holders), or equivalent cash	Rs. 5 or Rs. 2 rice	Rs. 10	Rs. 18 in cash or in kind (rice or labour)	Rs. 2 Institutions Rs. 6- Individuals	Rs. 2 or Rs. 5
Number of members	At least 75% of households (23 villages covered) Total insured 14,390	75,000	Approximately 1/5 to 1/6 of all house-holds in villages, (319 villages covered) 150 out of 175 households	150 out of 175 households in village	630 institutes total 350,000 students covered	6800
Member entitlement	Community care: free CHW services, drugs, and mobile (doctor +ANM) services. Hospital: free care for unphased illness episodes, 25% subsidy for anticipated illness episodes, e.g., pregnancy and chronic ailments	Community care: free CHW services and drugs. Free health centre services including MCH clinic. Hospital: free care after paying entrance fee up to ceiling of Rs. 1000	Community care: free services, subsidized drugs. Hospital: 50% subsidy	Dispensary: Free doctor consultations drugs at cost. Free periodic public health activities	Polyclinic/ regional clinics: free consultations, drugs, diagnostic tests, operations, bed stay at nominal charges	Outpatient clinic: free consultations, drugs at cost, free MCH care

Contd....

Features	*Sevagram*	*RAHA*	*Tribovandas Foundation*	*Goalpara*	*Students Health Home*	*SSSS*
Non-member entitlement	Non-members not entitled to use community health services	Non-members charged for drugs (over cost), not entitled to attend MCH clinic	Non-members have same emoluments to community services as members but not hospital care	Non-members charged for drugs (over cost)	Non-members not entitled to avail of services	Non-members are not entitled to avail the services
Management of fund	VHW responsible for membership collections, Collections once a year at harvest time. Compulsory that 75% of villages covered.	Individual health centres responsible for membership collections. Collections once a year. New members waiting period 2 months before services entitlements Rs. 3 retained by centre, Rs. 2 to RAHA for referral fund.	VHW services responsible for membership collections. Collected once a year at times-bonus payments distributed (non-adult society members can also enroll in scheme)	Village health communities-funds collections once a year.	Institutions enrolled once a year. Individuals ongoing (no waiting period)	Able to enroll through the year. No waiting period between enrollment and service entitlements.

Source: Dave [1991].

equitable health financing mechanism for the workers in informal sector. Various other terms are used with regards to community health insurance (CHI), including micro health insurance and local health insurance. The benefit of CHI lies in keeping transaction cost low, in formulating a scheme suited to community needs, in influencing health behaviour through health education and affecting the supply health care. CHI programmes offer best aspiration for cutting down financial burden caused by sickness to a large segment of the low-income groups. This scheme is purely based on non-profit making motive, which is intended for the workers informal sector and involve s repayment and the pooling of resources to cover the cost of health related matters. Often the schemes are operated by a hospital and intended at households of the surrounding area and membership is voluntary rather than compulsory. A survey of existing literature on health insurance suggested approaches to community financing. The conventional method to community financing was considered to be inapt and forced *Sewagram* to fashion its responses in the light of its own observations and experiences (Table 6.3).

Several NGOs and governments have initiated micro-credit schemes for vulnerable groups to crash the vicious circle of poverty, malnutrition, disease, low productivity, and low income. Micro-credit is now considered not only an effective tool for poverty reduction but also used as an instrument for empowerment of the poor, particularly the women. This operation creates income to the poor by extending them small credits for self-employment and other economic activities. However, it was soon realised that loan repayments by these groups were much below the expected level. The experience suggested that ill health and expenditure on treatment and associated consumption needs were the prime reasons for defaulting on repayments. To plug the erosion of income of borrowers

Table 6.3
Approaches to Community Financing

Conventional approach	*Sewagram experience*
It does little to promote equally, can place great burden on the poor and the sick, and suffers from poor selection.	The principle of contribution according to capacity, but services according to need, developed an egalitarian system, which does not suffer from poor selection.
It lacks stability and needs some external support to mobalise and sustain community efforts.	The acceptability and affordability of the scheme resulted in stability of revenue and willing community involvement on a sustainable basis.
It favours the creation of those health facilities for which there is high local demand, rather than meeting professionally perceived needs.	Doctors prefer not to over-medicate as the hospital has to raise 25 per cent of its own expenditure.
It carries the danger of an excessive use of facilities.	Also as the remaining 75 per cent of the funds is assured to the professionals, they do not succumb to whimsical local demands for tonics and injections.
It is never easy to sell the concept among poor people.	The facilities are primarily controlled by professionals and not by the people, thus avoiding chance of excessive use.
It tends to benefit the community more than individual and hence there could be greater reluctance to participate.	The need for and affordability of the scheme are strong selling points. Sewagram's insurance scheme is oriented more towards individual as there is an element of risk sharing and hence there is little reluctance to participate.

Source: Jajoo [2000].

on health care needs, some NGOs such as Grameen Bank in Bangladesh and the Self-Employed Women Association (SEWA) in India have initiated health insurance schemes for their members. The Grameen Bank Health Programme .was started in 1994 with the objectives to adopt preventive measures against diseases, to arrange for treatment at minimum cost, and to build a non-profit primary health care system. Under this scheme the borrowers pay a fixed annual amount of 60 *Taka* per family as premium and a very petty sum at the time of using the facility. The scheme over time has proven to meet the desired objectives (Rahman 2000). In India, SEWA is a trade union of 2,15,000 women workers of the informal sector. It organizes them towards the goals of full employment and self-reliance at the household level. Full employment includes social security, which in turn incorporates insurance. SEWA's experience repeatedly revealed that despite women's efforts to come out of poverty through enhanced employment opportunities and increased income, they were still vulnerable to various crises in their lives. These prevented them from leading a life free of poverty. The crises they continue to face are death of a breadwinner, accidental damage to and destruction of their homes and work equipment, and sickness. Maternity too often becomes a crisis for a woman, especially if she is poor, malnourished, and lives in a remote area. One of the SEWA studies observed that women identified sickness of themselves or a family member as the major stress event in their lives. It was also a major cause of indebtedness among women. The health insurance programme was, from the start, linked to SEWA's primary health care programme, which include occupational health services. Thus, insured members also have access to preventive and curative health care with health education. Health insurance accounts for the majority of claims and for 50 per cent of the premium paid out to the insurance programme by SEWA members. The scheme was introduced by the SEWA Bank in March 1992 with an initial enrolment of 7000 women from Ahmedabad city (Chatterjee and Vyas 1997). Later on it was extended to cover rural woman members from nine districts of Gujarat. Now its enrolment is 30,000 women, of which 50 per cent is from rural areas. Health insurance is an integral part of the insurance programme of SEWA. The major motivation behind the initiation of a health insurance scheme for women is that maintenance of an active health seeking behaviour is a vital component for ensuring a good quality life and women tend to place a low priority to their health care needs. The poor women's health is most vulnerable both because of their unhygienic living conditions as well as the burden of bearing children. And persistent poor health of such workers costs them in terms of loss of working days and the corresponding incomes. The coverage of the SEWA health insurance programme includes maternity coverage, hospitalization coverage for a wide range of diseases, and insurance for occupational health related illnesses and other diseases specific to women (Table 6.4). SEWA's health insurance scheme functions in co-ordination with Life Insurance Corporation of India (LIC) and New India Assurance Company (NIAC). SEWA has integrated the schemes of LIC and NIAC into a comprehensive health insurance package to address women's basic needs. The claimants are the needy health-benefits seekers and as the insurance is an additional benefit, the beneficiaries willingly pay the premium. Most of the insurers opt for fixed deposit of Rs. 500 or Rs. 700 (depending upon the type of coverage) with the SEWA Bank and the interest accrual goes towards annual payment of premium. It is the large membership and assets of the SEWA Bank that has made possible the provision of the insurance coverage at low premium.

Table 6.4
Type of Coverage Under SEWA Scheme

Provider	*Description of coverage*	*Coverage amount (Rs.)*	*Premium (Rs.)*
New India Assurance	Accidental death of the woman member	10,000	3.50
	Loss of assets		
	Accidental death of a member's husband	10,000	3.50
SEWA	Loss during riots, fire, floods, theft, etc.:		
	(a) of work equipment	2000	8.00
	(b) of the housing unit	3000	
	Health Insurance (Including cover age for:	1200	30.00 (10)
	(a) gynecological ailments		
	(b) occupational health related diseases)		(5)
	Maternity Benefits	300	-
Life Insurance Corporation of India	Natural death	3000	15.00
	Accidental death	25,000	

Note: Total premium for the entire package is Rs. 60 plus Rs. 5 as service charge.

The comprehensive review of the existing health insurance schemes for informal sector in India describes that several programmes indulge to economically lower segment of the population. The voluntary health insurance plan, which covers only hospitalization expenses, is too expensive for the informal sector workers to get enrolled. There are various community-based and self-financing schemes but, given the massive health care needs, the coverage of population by them is just not adequate. The proportion of population covered by any health insurance scheme is minute, let alone those employed in informal sector. The market for health insurance is growing at a substantial rate, though. At this stage, it may be worthwhile to abridge the experience with health insurance of select Asian and Latin American countries to understand what lessons can be learnt by India. There have been commendable efforts in developing health insurance models by these countries whose per capita incomes are well below those of the developed countries. The specific experiences of China, Thailand, Indonesia, Sri Lanka, Chile, Uruguay, Colombia, Brazil, and Argentina are worth mentioning. China stands out as an example where insurance has been successful in covering a large part of the population both in rural and urban areas. The Chinese expenditure is characterised by high total expenditure, low government expenditure and heavy dependence on insurance financing. There are two kinds of coverage which are in practice in China namely, labour insurance medical coverage for State-owned enterprise workers and retired persons, and free medical service which caters to workers and retired persons of government agencies and parties and non-profit institutions. A noteworthy feature of China's health care system is the coverage of rural population through various kinds of schemes, which have been designed in accordance with the local economic conditions and public opinion. China's system of health care certainly scores better compared to some of its Asian counterparts like India and Indonesia. Thailand has four different kinds of health care financing programmes namely, voluntary health schemes, mandatory schemes, social welfare schemes, and fringe benefit schemes. The target population of each of these schemes varies in terms of their place of residence (rural/urban) and employment status (formal sector/informal sector). The coverage of population in the informal sector, especially in rural areas is, however, far from a enviable level. In fact, 41 per cent of the population, which is not covered by health insurance scheme largely, consists of subsistence farmers, self-employed, rural workers, and urban dwellers engaged in informal sector activity such as street vending and small-scale commercial undertakings. Despite this under-coverage, the experiment with the health card scheme seems to have worked. The health-card scheme is designed for delivering health care services to the workers in the informal sector where assessing incomes is problematic. The health-card scheme was initiated primarily with the objective of improving health among the rural population. Indonesia, with a very low level of government expenditure and negligible insurance spending, fares the worst (among the countries under comparison) as far as health outcomes are concerned. In the Asian group of countries, Sri Lanka too (like China) emerges as a good performer. However, the pattern of health care expenditure between the two greatly varies. While China relies substantially on insurance spending, Sri Lanka's health care expenditure is characterised by high government, low private, and low insurance expenditures. The pattern of health care expenditure in Latin American countries varies according to the size of the country (both in terms of population and geographical size) and the income level. Taking a larger perspective, there are mainly two types of managed competition, which are emerging in this region where government is the sponsor and where private employers are playing the role of sponsor. The former type is followed in countries like Chile, Uruguay, and Colombia. In Chile, for instance, 73 per cent of the population is covered by public health care whereas the remaining 27 per cent are enrolled into the ISPRAE, a private insurance plan. Colombia too has a system of mixed public funding and managed competition, which has not only increased the coverage but also made the system more equitable. In fact, Colombia's health care system has been hailed as one of the most successful ones in the region. Brazil has three distinct systems being availed of by three different income classes namely, public system primarily by informal sector and low-income workers, private supplementary medicine by formal sector and middle-income workers, and direct out-of-pocket payments by high-income workers. Argentina's health delivery system is mixed and a large number of private insurance plans. While the broad goals and objectives of the health care system in the reviewed countries remain equity and efficiency in the delivery of health care, yet there are variations in the design of programmes, role of government, etc. In the Asian group of countries, China and Sri Lanka, with their success in the health arena, do pose as examples worth emulating but it needs to be noted that each of them follows a different pattern. In Sri Lanka, there is a dominance of government spending in the health sector whereas insurance spending is substantial in China. In the Indian case, the effort can be two-directional. Government health spending can be improved in terms of the amount spent as well as efficiency of expenditure. The latter is, however, more important. The widespread introduction of low user fees in government hospitals can improve the provision of basic health services. A mix of government expenditure as well private insurance is possible but the amount of premium to be collected from workers in the informal sector remains a moot question. This becomes all the more important when the share of informal sector workers is more than 90 per cent and it is not easy to make an assessment of their income. The Chinese model throws some light on how risk sharing can be made workable even in rural areas where incomes are not too low. The India-China comparison has always been a subject of debate because of their similarities in terms of geographical size, population, and low levels of income. China has exceeded India as far as the achievements in the area of health are concerned. China's basic indicators of infant mortality rate, life expectancy, and maternal mortality are far more favourably placed as compared to those of India. Thailand's health-card scheme has been another pioneering attempt towards promoting grass-root participation and management skills (Gumber 2002).

EXTENDING COVERAGE

There are several important issues concerning formulating, designing and operationalizng an affordable health insurance scheme for the poor in informal sector. Before introducing a unique plan, wide-ranging designs in different settings can be tried out on a pilot basis. The critical points and steps to be considered in this process are as follows (Gumber 2002).

(a) Defining Benefit Package

The types of benefits to be included are:

(i) *Inpatient Care:* The event is unpredictable but rare and the cost of treatment is either unaffordable or payment pushes people, even the better off, into indebtedness and poverty.

(ii) *Outpatient Care:* Insurance is generally not well suited to routine ambulatory care because its requirements tend to be reasonably predictable and are of relatively low cost and people might be expected to meet these costs out of their pockets as they go along without too much hardship. Most people, however, do prefer the inclusion of at least those services (diagnostic and clinical) having a bearing on their pockets.

(iii) *Chronic Care:* Insurance is also poorly placed to meet the needs of chronic care as such conditions, although of high cost, are not unpredictable. As long as members of a scheme may be willing to subsidize others in rare times of extreme need, they may be unwilling to heavily subsidize them on a regular basis. This is not to say that providing protection for

those with chronic illness is not important, but just that insurance is not the best way of doing it.

(iv) *Maternity Care:* Another area that generates considerable discussion is that of the possible inclusion of deliveries in the package. It is possible to argue that while mothers have nine months to plan to meet the financial costs of normal delivery and should be expected to do so themselves, a scheme might include emergency deliveries which are rarer but expensive. If schemes do decide to include outpatient care and chronic care they must expect premiums to rise. Also, experience tends to suggest that women groups do want deliveries to be included. If so, the costs of the scheme may rise and again a future requirement might be to include all antenatal care. Individual schemes may wish to deviate from these broad principles. One option might be to offer greater protection to the poorest in the group by perhaps offering them greater benefits, i.e., to cover the cost of ambulatory care where this benefit is not enjoyed by better off members. Alternatively, schemes could decide to meet the non-medical costs of treatment (e. g., transport costs) or they may even wish to extend benefits beyond just health care to cover loss of income, though this is unlikely and should only be considered when there is a demonstrated record of economic sustainability and ability to pay. Another possible approach is to consider whether referrals to the more specialized facilities are to be included. Should a scheme's benefits be restricted to secondary hospitals or should referral for, say, specialist cancer treatment or heart surgery be allowed? This could potentially be very high cost and could drain the scheme, resources. What is an appropriate role for the State? The government would presumably wish to give some freedom to determine the benefit package but may wish to insist that certain elements be included, e.g., inpatient and preventive care. Also a minimal benefit package should be defined so as to ensure delivery of only cost-effective services.

(b) Deciding on a Panel of Providers

If services are free there is little point in getting insurance. If most of the costs are in the form of unofficial fees, again health insurance can do little to help. Health insurance only makes sense when fees are being charged and this may rule out involvement with government facilities. However, fees may differ significantly from government facilities, where services may be free, to NGO providers to expensive for-profit providers. Obviously the higher the fees, the higher will be the premiums needed for a scheme to break even, but also the greater are potential benefits from health insurance. The question is whether the services should be restricted to just one provider or whether members should have choices. This depends largely on what members want and where they are currently getting their services but the decision does have some implications as set out below. In some areas, especially rural and hilly areas, there may be little choice. Such an approach is perhaps easier to implement, although lack of competition reduces any pressure on the provider to improve the services. In urban areas, there may be a number of potential providers. Dealing with a larger number may be more difficult from a managerial point of view but does offer better potential for driving up quality. A scheme offering a choice of providers must include incentives for members to access the quality of care they need in the cheapest setting. One way to do this is to charge higher co-payments for higher cost providers.

(c) Type of Membership and Population Coverage

This includes whether the scheme would cover just the villagers, slum dwellers, poor, occupation groups, thrift and credit groups, select geographic unit, workers, women, or adult groups. Unit costs will differ if switching over from individual to household memberships because children and other dependents (elderly) have different health needs than the working population. Clearly, on the one hand the more are the people that are covered, the higher are the premiums per household, but on the other hand there is a reduction in adverse selection.

(d) Reducing Moral Hazard and Preventing Adverse Selection

Although the ultimate decision should be down to the group itself it is advisable that unless the majority of members join (ideally all) there are likely to be problems. Ideally one should cover the entire village or panchayat or settlement and make the scheme compulsory while covering minimal benefit package. If services are free to members once they have paid a premium they have a strong incentive to use services even if their need is not great. One-way of preventing such overuse (also called moral hazard) is to charge co-payments–a small amount charged when services are used. Although far less than the user fees, this would at least provide a deterrent to unnecessary use. Also, on the provider side there are incentives for over-treatment and also the possibility of fraudulent practices as numbers and providers collaborate to falsify claims. One should aim at creating incentives for cost-effective treatment, i.e., preventing unnecessary use of services and ensuring services are of the appropriate quality provided at reasonable cost. Approaches exist to contain, if not prevent, such practices totally. Members themselves would be expected to monitor the use themselves through peer pressure; it may also be possible to compare utilization between groups to identify areas where overuse may be possible. Any managing organization could monitor this issue.

(e) Organizational Arrangements

Management will be important at all stages of preparation, design, implementation, and evaluation. One approach might be to contract an NGO to take on this role. They might carry out the initial groundwork and be responsible for monitoring schemes, perhaps even for negotiating special discounted rates with providers. If the groups are small, the managing agency may wish to introduce an additional element of risk pooling by taxing schemes and redistributing these funds to schemes in need. The role of evaluation would, of course, be given to another institution. A managing institution, however, would require special skills in the areas of community participation/community liaison/ marketing, bookkeeping and financial analysis, monitoring, access to medical expertise (to validate treatment decisions) and possibly in providing preventive care directly (funded through premiums).

(f) Payment Systems

There are a number of options here. In short, the approach should be as simple as possible and not open to fraud. Funds could be retained within the age group or held at the facility (if they can be trusted). Members might be given a card with their photograph on it and be exempted at the facility with the scheme reimbursing the provider afterwards. Alternatively, the member might be expected to make payment up front and be reimbursed by the scheme later–though this may present a significant barrier to some.

(g) The Task of Government

A number of important roles emerge for government in the development of a health insurance scheme, which include financing, management, training, monitoring, and evaluation. First of all, it would be important to carry out a mapping exercise which would include the following: identifying the nature and activities of the target groups, assessing their knowledge of, and interest in, health insurance and carry out advocacy and training as necessary through workshops and door-to-door campaigns, identify interested groups for the pilot project; carry out willingness-to-pay survey and design the cost benefit package; carry out a baseline survey on current health practices in the pilot project area and also in control groups to obtain approximate initial administration costs. It might be reasonable to provide schemes with government funds to meet the initial start-up costs. Those would not be significant as the approach would be paper based. Although an ongoing subsidy is probably unwarranted schemes would be expected to be self-supporting with the benefit package tailored to meet what people are willing to pay in the short term a subsidy might be justified. Government can also stimulate the interest in the schemes and guarantee interest so that the people can learn the benefits of insurance, a concept many will be unfamiliar with. It can also provide an extra incentive to well designed schemes – the subsidies may be made available to schemes which incorporate elements of best practices (one approach may be to cover 50 per cent of premiums for a fixed period of two years). If government wishes to evaluate schemes with a view to their replication it is important that the schemes are developed in a variety of settings (urban/rural with varied access to types of health facilities and socio-economic population groups). Otherwise they will leave themselves open to criticism that they only work in particular circumstances.

It is also important to be clear about what the schemes are intended to achieve so that there can be some basis for evaluation.

SUMMARY

Health insurance has gained amplified importance as a financing tool in meeting health care facilities to the poor in the informal sector. Community based health insurance is more useful mechanism for providing insurance to the poor. However the approach of the government is to support voluntary insurance rather than to widen the existing social insurance schemes. Social insurance may be better way of providing health protection to the low-income groups but alternative straightforward approaches to the people below the poverty line is needed.

REFERENCES

Ahmad, E., Dreze, J. and Sen, A. (eds.) (1991), *Social Security in Developing Countries*. Clarendon Press, Oxford.

Chatterjee, M. and Vyas, J. (1997), *Organizing Insurance for Women Workers: The SEWA Experience.* Self-Employed Women's Association (SEWA), Ahmedabad.

Datta, R.C. (1998), Public Action, Social Security and Unorganised Sector. *Economic and Political Weekly*, XXXIII (22) : L2-L5.

Dave, P. (1991), Community and Self-Financing in Voluntary Health Programmes in India. *Health Policy and Planning*, 6 (1): 20–31.

Guhan, S. (1994), Social Security Options for Developing Countries. *International Labour Review*, 133 (1): 35-53.

Gumber, A. (2002), *Health Insurance for the Informal Sector: Problems and Prospects.* Working Paper No. 90, Indian Council for Research on International Economic Relations, New Delhi.

Jajoo, U.N. (2000), Health Insurance for the Poor: Innovations in Primary Health Care. In: R. Jhabvala *et al.* (eds). *The*

Unorganised Sector: Work Security and Social Protection. Sage Publications, New Delhi.

Prabhu, K.S. (2001), *Economic Reforms and Social Development*. Sage Publications, New Delhi.

Rahman, K. (2000), Poverty, Micro-Credit and Health: What Role Can WHO Play? *WHO Regional Health Forum*, 4 (1 & 2): 68–80.

Sarkar, S. (2004a), Extending Social Security Coverage to the Informal Sector in India. *Social Change*, 34 (4): 122-130.

Sarkar, S. (2004b), Theorising in Informal Sector: Concept and Context. *Social Action*, 54 (40): 359-373.

Chapter - 7

Getting Rid of Girl Child Labour

INTRODUCTION

The issue relating to child labour is a global phenomenon. In India the incidence of child labour is in almost all sector. It has been estimated that children working in India in between 60 and 115 million the highest number in the world, which is 25 per cent of the working children of the world. In developing countries the number working children between the age of 5 and 14 is projected about 250 million, at least 120 million of them work full time (World Bank 1999). The majority of the children working in rural areas engage in agricultural activities while urban children lead to work in service and manufacturing. Although official statistics suggest that more boys work than girls the main difference is that boys tend to work in more visible types of employment while girls perform a low paid household jobs. While this difference is taken into consideration, boys and girls work in similar proportions. Whatever be the proportions existing in India, child labour contributing significantly to Indian economy is worth investigating. Presently children are being moved away from their families to work in hazardous and exploitative activities in the informal sectors like match, firework, brick kiln, glassware, carpet, shoe making etc. On account of more working hour in adverse conditions, most of child labour face chronic health hazards such as cuts, loss of body parts, burns, skin diseases, sight or hearing loss and acute respiratory illness. There are two groups of factors, which determine the decision to become active in the informal sector, more specifically, the structural as well as opportunity factors. The structural factors consist of financial pressure, socio-psychological pressure and institutional constraints. The opportunity factors consist of individual background, skills, education, living condition or non-individual components, environment, values, standards etc. (Sarkar 2004). Estimates of child labour range from 11.28 million to what constitutes the 'nowhere' children that some non-governmental organizations claim to be the alternative estimation of potential child labour over 100 million (Chaudhuri 1996). This is even more so in the context of the girl child who has the added disadvantage of non-recognition of most of her work carried out as an unpaid, household member. This has to be kept in mind while presenting the official estimates of girl child labour across the country (Visaria 1999). According to 1991 Census, nearly 5 million girls are working either as main or marginal workers. Of the 76 million girls in the population among the age group 5-14 years, there will be many more silent workers. Among the main workers, there are more than 3 million girls and nearly 5 million boys at the all India level. Another 1.6 million girls are categorized as marginal workers, while only half a million boys fall in this category. The child work participation rate in India [i.e. child workers (main plus marginal) as a proportion of the total population in the age group 5-14 years] is 7 for males and 6 for females. Variation in the female child work participation rate (FCWPR) is more than that of the male children across the states. From very insignificant levels in Kerala and Punjab, the proportion of working female children ranges up to 14 per cent in Andhra Pradesh. Other states where the FCWPR is reported to be high are Mizoram, Madhya Pradesh, Karnataka, Maharashtra and Rajasthan (Table 7.1).

Table 7.1
State-wise Child Work Participation Rates

State	*Child Work Participation Rate*		
	Person	*Male*	*Female*
Andhra Pradesh	12	11	14
Arunachal Pradesh	6	5	7
Assam	6	7	4
Bihar	4	5	3
Goa	2	2	2
Gujarat	7	6	8
Haryana	3	4	2
Himachal Pradesh	5	4	6
Karnataka	11	11	11
Kerala	1	1	1
Madhya Pradesh	10	9	11
Maharashtra	8	7	10
Manipur	5	4	5
Meghalaya	9	10	8
Mizoram	11	10	12
Nagaland	6	5	7
Orissa	6	7	6
Punjab	4	6	1
Rajasthan	8	6	10
Sikkim	5	5	5
Tamil Nadu	6	5	7
Tripura	2	3	2
Uttar Pradesh	4	5	3
West Bengal	5	7	3
India	6	7	6

Source: Computed from *Census of India* [1991].

The female to male ratio among total child workers reveals the number of girls working for every 1000 male child workers. In the areas where the sex ratios among child workers surpass 1000, this reflects the discriminatory treatment meted out to girls and their excessive use in labour activities as opposed to boys in the region. Girls are mostly marginal workers, while more boys figure as main workers. The states where girls predominate as main workers over boys are Arunachal Pradesh, Manipur, Himachal Pradesh, Goa, Nagaland, Maharashtra, Mizoram, Sikkim, Andhra Pradesh and Tamil Nadu. Among the marginal workers, girls exceed boys in all states except for Kerala and Nagaland (Table 7.2).

Table 7.2
State-wise Sex Ratios Among Total Population, Main and Marginal Workers

State	*Sex Ratios Among*		
	Total population (5-14 years)	*Main workers*	*Marginal workers*
Andhra Pradesh	948	1040	3300
Arunachal Pradesh	933	1328	2958
Assam	964	336	3095
Bihar	880	335	3554
Goa	968	1201	1966
Gujarat	925	586	7960
Haryana	860	300	4120
Himachal Pradesh	966	1273	1892
Karnataka	981	830	3338
Kerala	983	751	985
Madhya Pradesh	926	758	3066
Maharashtra	941	1156	2746
Manipur	966	1281	1736
Meghalaya	983	702	1674
Mizoram	986	1125	1090
Nagaland	955	1165	962
Orissa	987	494	3799
Punjab	883	80	5453
Rajasthan	888	827	4413
Sikkim	980	1058	1516
Tamil Nadu	955	1033	6100
Tripura	960	512	2521
Uttar Pradesh	858	269	2777
West Bengal	963	323	1710
India	918	638	3281

Source: Calculated from *Census of India* [1991].

Table 7.3
Sex Ratio Among Child Workers and Number of Districts with Higher Number of Girls Working

State	Sex ratio among child workers (SRCW)	No. of districts with SRCW> 1000	Total No. of districts
Andhra Pradesh	1127	19	23
Arunachal Pradesh	1391	11	11
Assam	563	4	23
Bihar	522	6	42
Goa	1343	2	2
Gujarat	1129	13	19
Haryana	536	3	16
Himachal Pradesh	1521	12	12
Karnataka	1039	13	20
Kerala	792	3	14
Madhya Pradesh	1075	27	45
Maharashtra	1426	29	30
Manipur	1344	8	8
Meghalaya	776	–	5
Mizoram	1107	3	3
Nagaland	1159	6	7
Orissa	866	6	13
Punjab	160	–	12
Rajasthan	1443	24	27
Sikkim	1081	3	4
Tamil Nadu	1205	18	21
Tripura	697	–	3
Uttar Pradesh	465	7	63
West Bengal	456	1	17
India	879	218	440

Source: Calculated from *Census of* India [1991]

The burden of work on girls is higher in the districts where the participation of girls in work exceeds that of the boys. Hence it is these districts that are identified in this analysis. Of the 440 districts belonging to 24 states, 218 districts have a higher number of girls working than boys in the age group 5-14 years, either as main or marginal workers (Table 7.3). A larger number of girl children are working in all districts of Himachal Pradesh, Arunachal Pradesh, Manipur, Mizoram and Goa. Other states where almost all the districts record a higher participation of girls are Andhra Pradesh, Rajasthan, Maharashtra, Sikkim, Nagaland and Tamil Nadu. More than half the number of districts in the states of Gujarat, Karnataka and Madhya Pradesh also display comparatively higher work participation levels of girl children.

POVERTY AND CHILD LABOUR

Poverty is one of the most fundamental issues, and urgently needs to be addressed. Moving people out of poverty forms a basis of much international development policy. The way poverty is conceptualized has changed in recent years. When people considering as 'poor' describe their own situation, they consider that their well-being is not enough, for example, they feel a lack of access to sufficient levels of food, water, clothing, shelter, sanitation, healthcare, and education. The change in conceptualization of poverty has lead to new ways of addressing moving people out of poverty. Although there is still an emphasis on income generation through increasing the opportunities for the poor women and girl child to participate in markets, there has been a broadening of strategies to enable the empowerment of poor women. Empowerment aims to address the inequalities, including gender inequalities, which prevent people from influencing policies and interventions, which affect their lives. Statistical exercises based on different sets of data have established that child labour is positively related, among other factors, to poverty, education, agriculture, and the overall work participation ratio. Girls are also preferred in specific sectors to undertake piece rate, home-based, contractual work as in the case of beedi making, bricks making, making matches, fireworks, agarbatti making, bangle making and so on, or in the case of tasks involving sorting, packaging, labelling, etc.

(Chandrasekhar 1997). Increasing the security of poor people by addressing the factors, which create their vulnerability, has become a part of international development thinking. How is informal activity seen in the new approaches to poverty alleviation? Illness reduces the ability of poor people to improve their livelihoods and increases their vulnerability, not only preventing adults from working effectively but also negatively effecting children's learning by keeping them from school. The informality-poverty nexus has distinct gender characteristics. Within households, where there are adult men and women, the gendered division of labour generally allocates to women the responsibility for household tasks provision related to their spheres of influence in the household. They are often supported in this work by girls and sometimes boys, who can be kept out of school thereby damaging their own future livelihood choices. Women's access to decision-making within the household and community is restricted, limiting their ability to influence processes and resource allocation. Poor men and women do not necessarily become poor in the same ways, for example, a man might loose his job, and a woman, who has always depended on her husband for financial support, may become a widow, forcing her to start looking for a paying job later in her life, which she might be ill equipped to do so. Men and women have different ways of adopting strategies for addressing their poverty, men are more easily able to migrate while women stay put managing the household and creating home-based enterprise they can run from own house. Therefore, the informalisation strategies that are intended to assist people to move out of poverty must take these gender aspects into account. The cultural explanation is not necessarily distinct from the poverty explanation. It has often been argued that child work was essential to the survival of the children and their families. It is indeed obvious that, by and large, poverty is an important reason why children work. If they were not working, the survival of the entire family could be at stake. Child labour as a matter of fact can be beneficial to the child, not only in terms of the preparation for the tasks of adulthood, but also in terms of the direct improvement of their health condition. Since labour adds to the family income, it will add to the nutritional intake of the young worker, and the morbidity levels of the working child may even be lower than the levels prevailing among comparable counterparts. With these considerations in mind, it is not uncommon to divide child labour into four categories, from intolerable to hazardous to neutral and ending up with varieties of child work, which may even, have a positive impact on the future adult. Acute poverty is usually advanced as a reason for sending children to work. This is obviously an explanation that requires neither substantiation nor verification. It is common sense to accept that the poorer the family, the poorer the district, the poorer the country, the higher would be the incidence of child labour. A closer observation, however, suggests that this is the case in a restricted sense only. The first problem with this explanation is that poverty is difficult to define and that poverty in any case refers not just to economic poverty. There are certain thresholds below which people will find it difficult to survive. These thresholds are defined by nutrition, sanitation, health and shelter. At the level of deprivation, below these minimum thresholds, there is not much of an option between work and non-work. Deprivation often comes as a shock effect: the dead or severe illness of the adult breadwinner has often been documented to be a direct cause underlying child labour. Poverty defined as human deprivation goes to the root of the child labour problem. Child labour is a source of income of poor families. Studies show that a child's income accounted for between 34 and 37 per cent of the total household income. Therefore a child labour's income is important to the livelihood of the vulnerable family. There are several reasons for growing tendency of child labour in India. However poverty, possibly, may be considered as major reason, which contributes to harmful child labour in India. The percentage of population of India living in the poverty is high. Poverty has an obvious relationship with child labour and studies reveal a positive correlation between child labour and poverty. For poor, there are a few sources of bank loans and other credit sources, here enters local money lenders, parents exchange their children to local money lenders with an agreed money. As the earnings of bonded child labourers are less than the interest on loans, these bonded children are forced to work until interest on loan accumulates. A bonded child can only be released after his parents make a lump sum payment, which is extremely difficult for the poor. Although poverty is cited as the major cause of child labour, but it is not merely determinant, inadequate number of schools expenses of schooling and even attitudes of parents also contribute to child labour. Some parents feel that children should work in order to develop skills in job market instead of taking advantages of formal education. The other reasons are high average rate of illiteracy (52.11 per cent, 1991 census) among the parents which push their children to engage in child labour force in lieu of providing them education and other facilities, insufficiency of protective legislation and regulations and lack of strong child labour unions in India. In short socio-economic conditions in India contribute to greater incidence of child labour. For the sake of future of all children, it is an immediate necessary to ensure sustainable economic growth and development especially in country like India where child labour is on the rise. It relates to many factors that cannot be quantified or streamlined into econometric exercises.

Deprivation relates to exclusion, to vulnerability and to ignorance as much as to physical weakness and lack of property assets. Children living under such conditions, especially when a shock event has torn normal family life apart, will work in order to survive. By working, they find an individual answer to calamities for which society does not take responsibility. Poverty, as it as traditionally defined, usually combines a number of factors such as the existence of many children per households, with low literacy levels and with a horizon of low-paid and unskilled jobs, open to child labour (Lieten 2002).

OBJECTIVE AND METHODOLOGY

The objective of the study is to delve into the girl child labour process in brick kilns, employment and working conditions, socio-economic security and how they coalesce paid work with other responsibilities. In the present endavour emphasis is given more on socio-economic characteristics of girl child labour associations in the kilns based on the primary data collection. This study is based on observations, interviews and a sample of 65 girl child workers from a total of five brick kilns in North Bengal region. The stratified random sampling method has been adopted while collecting sample workers.

FINDINGS

The brick kiln is mainly a small-scale manufacturing unit where manual labour and hard work is predominant. There are 50,000 brick kilns all over India employing average 100 workers – male workers counted only who are on the muster rolls of the employers (Gupta 2003). Workers of brick kilns comprise of vulnerable section of the society mostly women and children. In rural settings poor families often send their children to work in the informal sectors in order to increasing household income and ensuring family survival.

The manufacturing process of bricks consists of moulding, carrying unbaked dried bricks, baking and stacking. The female labour is preferred for moulding and often carrying bricks, while the male workers carry out other activities. Girl child labour is especially engaged in moulding. The bricks workers are employed by the principal employer or by the contractor. The wage rate for bricks making largely varies from one kiln to another. The principal employers or manufacturers after making discussion with the concerned trade union settle the wage rate. So, there is every possibility of revision of wage rate. In brick kilns, female and girl child workers are mostly preferred because of the limitation of alternative job opportunities for them and moreover, they can be easily exploited by the contractors in paying a lower wage rate. The wage rate for the girl child workers irrespective of nature of work varies from an average of Rs.60 to Rs.75 per 1,000 bricks and working hour ranges between 8 to10. It is observed from the study that among the girl child, the illiterates constituted 27.7 per cent. 46.2 per cent of them had school going experience. The bricks workers may be recruited by the principal employer or contractor. The survey discloses that only 4.6 per cent of the total children were employed by the principal employers or manufactures, while most of the girl child labour were recruited by the contractors. The demand for contract employment was on the rise because of limited opportunity to work as direct factory labour. The economic compulsion was the main reasons of the children behind taking up bricks making as their livelihood. It is interestingly to note that most of the girl child labourers enter the labour force for meeting own educational expenses. The survey shows the responses about work experiences of the girl child workers in bricks making. The respondents were asked to recall the age at which they began working. 29.2 per cent of the workers reported that they had been working for less than a year, while 64.6 per cent of the workers had an experience of 2-3 years. The majority of child workers joined the labour force at the age of 9-11 years old.

The respondents were badly affected by fumes of the kiln. It is found that some health related problems like skin diseases, asthma increased with age and number of years work. 23.1 per cent of the girl workers had no major health problems except the problems like headache, shoulder pain, leg pain etc. All the rest had faced acute health problems due to inhalation of dust of baked clay. The girl child workers had to do simultaneously their own household task. They had to combine wage work with their domestic responsibilities. It is found that in addition to bricks making, the workers had to do help their mother in sundry household task. The girl workers had nearly full responsibilities on the activities like washing utensils and water collection. The contribution of child workers to their families was in no way negligible. It is observed that in the economic sphere the status of most of the workers was similar as that of other members in their family. 53.8 per cent of the workers contributed more than Rs 400 per month to their family. Most of the girl workers contributed in the range of Rs 500 to Rs 700 per month and majority were found to spend a part of their earnings for their education.

SUMMARY

Therefore girl child labour is a significant problem in India. The prevalence of it is shown by the child work participation rates, which are higher in India than in other developing countries. The policies that reduce girl child labour have strong support on purely economic grounds. While children are sent to work at very young age for extended period they do not develop the skills necessary to earn higher wages later in life and a society loses needed human capital.

Several approaches in order to deducing girl child labour have been suggested. However our suggestions are:

- Increasing primary school enrollments tend to decrease girl child labour.
- Raising parental awareness of loss of human capital associated with girl child labour.
- By brute enforcing laws and regulations governing girl child labour.
- Providing support services to girl child labour.
- Targeting women self help group as a part of the getting rid of girl child labour.
- Launching rural energy entrepreneurship programme that improve the earning of the poor people may help to reduce girl child in long run.

REFERENCES

Chandrasekhar, C.P. (1997), The Economic Consequences of the Abolition of Child Labour: An Indian Case Study. *The Journal of Peasant Studies,* 24 (3): 137-79.

Chaudhuri, D.P. (1996), *Dynamic Profile of Child Labour in India 1951-1991.* ILO, New Delhi.

Gupta, J. (2003), Informal Labour in Brick Kilns: Need for Regulation. *Economic and Political Weekly*, XXXVIII (31): 3282-3292.

Lieten, G.K. (2002), Child Labour and Poverty: The Poverty of Analysis. *The Indian Journal of Labour Economics*, 45 (3): 451-464.

Sarkar, S. (2004), Theorising in Informal Sector: Concept and Context. S*ocial Action*, 54 (4) 356-373.

Visaria, P. (1999), Levels and Patterns of Female Employment, 1911-1994'. In T.S.Papola and A.N.Sharma (eds). *Gender and Employment in India*. Vikas Publising House, New Delhi.

World Bank (1999), *Entering 21st Century*. World Development Report 1999/2000, Washington DC.

Chapter - 8

Women, Environmental Pollution and Health

INTRODUCTION

A big section of planners and policymakers think that there are no serious environmental problems in the country. According to them, if however there be any, a variety of solutions exist. They often are of the opinion that government should come forward to implement the solution. As a remedial package minimization of public sector interference and maximization of government intervention, ensuring suitable prices for infrastructure and urban amenities through removal or reduction of subsidies, generating employment directly through anti-poverty programs, easing private and joint sector projects are being prescribed. However the ultimate solution is being sought through competent and transparent management of environmental projects. Although the desirability of growth is globally accepted and recognized, recent years have provided testimony to raising anxiety about whether environmental constraints will limit development or whether development will cause serious environmental degradation. A number of environmental problems are already very serious and call for immediate attention. Environmental threats evolve because of both resource depletion and negative externalities caused by development process and projects. With a view to achieving the object of sustainable development, it is inevitable to do with both types of problem adequately.

This paper is an attempt to present an overview of current status of environment in Indian context, raising also emerging critical issues like pollution and health linkage among rural women. The paper mainly delves into the damage to the physical and social environment with ultimate result that human hygiene may be deteriorate, economic productivity may be declined and pleasure satisfaction gained from any unspoiled environment often termed as its amenity value may also be absent to the present and future human welfare. The paper is organized as follows. Section II deals with land use, forest cover and pastures clubbing together can be said to constitute common property resource appear to have diminished both in quantity and also in quality and productivity. Section III states soil erosion and ill effects of water pollution on living beings. Disposal of solid waste continues to be unscientific and pressure of livestock on land having an adverse effect on regeneration capacity is focused on section IV. Section describes indoor and outdoor air pollution posing acute hygienic risks. The data and methodology of the field survey have been highlighted in section V and finding of the survey of field investigation has been presented in section VI. The role of Global Environmental Facility

(GEF) in supporting a list of measures to ensure global environment sustainability is indicated in section VII. The paper concludes that government should introduce environmental tax as a fiscal measure to curb degradation and it must consider implications of indigenous environmental policy decisions for other countries.

LAND USE, FOREST COVER AND PASTURES

Agriculture constitutes the major use of land in the country as a whole. Clubbing together net sown area and present fallow, it accounted for 48.7 per cent of total geographical area in 1958-59 and 51.3 per cent in 1995-96 in India. Though the proportion of land under agriculture increased by 2.6 per cent in India over this period, the proportion of land under forest with regard to legal status (not essentially under actual tree cover) enhanced in the country as a whole from 17.9 per cent to 22.4 per cent during the same period (Table 8.1).

Table 8.1
Land Use Pattern in India

	1958-59		*1995-96*	
	Area ('000 hectares)	*Percentage*	*Area ('000 hectares)*	*1993-94 Percentage*
Total geographical area	2,93,972	100	3,04,863	100
Forest	52,675	17.9	68,421	22.4
Non-agricultural use	13,563	4.6	22,035	7.2
Cultivable waste	20,610	7	14,468	4.7
Permanent pastures and grazing	13,112	4.5	11,176	3.7
Other fallows	12,286	4.2	9,703	3.2
Agricultural use	1,43,136	48.7	1,56,428	51.3

Note: Agricultural uses = Current fallows + net cultivated area

Source: Nadkani, M.V.1999. Environment in Karnataka–a status report. *Economic and Political Weekly*, XXXIV (9): 2736.

Forest on the other hand as a natural resource is not only aggregate of all trees but also a whole of the living and non-living elements which has a cultural and spiritual value. According to a release issued by the Food and Agriculture Organization of United Nations (1995) global forest, woodland and scrub cover decreased by 2 per cent or 100 million hectares during 1980s. In developing countries though the forest cover decreased by only 98.7

million hectares in 1980s, the loss of natural forest cover alone was 163 million hectares i.e. 8 per cent during the same period. In India despite the initiation of massive plantation programs the actual forest cover is coming down over the years. It has been projected that annual logging of closed forest in India during the period 1981-1990 is 42,000 hectares i.e. 1 per cent of closed forest. The Indian Remote Sensing Satellite imagery (1995) reveals that the extent of forest cover of the country was over 19 pert cent of the geographical area, but the imagery also discloses that less than 12 per cent was dense cover. Therefore this deforestation has a lot of ill effects like loss of sustainable logging potential and of erosion protection, watershed stability and carbon sequestration provided by the forests. Further loss of bio-diversity tends to potential loss of modern drugs and genetic resources.

Substantive pastures, cultivable wastes and other fallows combined together can be said to constitute common property resources used for grazing. According to official data, the proportion of such land reduced significantly from 15.7 per cent to 11.6 per cent between 1958-59 and 1995-96 in India. The role of such common property resources as a source of fodder had been decreasing over the years. With the growing trend of population in urban areas and economic development price of livestock products had increased significantly over the years. So trend from official data shows that common property resources appear to have slowed down both in quantity and also in quality and productivity.

SOIL EROSION AND WATER POLLUTION

Soil erosion is a principal problem affecting particularly in dry and rain fed areas. It reduces fertility of land owned by poor cultivators and invites drought. Apart from field productivity losses, soil erosion increases to costs such as river transport channels and other hydrologic investments. As far as soil conservation is concerned only 20.9 per cent out of total problem area of 52.2 per cent were taken into consideration up to 1992-93. So there is still a long path to go.

Besides water shortages add health hazards and it may be marked as ill effect of water degradation on productivity. It has already been estimated that by 2025 thirty-four countries including India will face water stress and of late about 29 countries are suffering from water scarcity. It is also expecting that number of people dwelling in water scare countries will increase from 132 million in 1990 to between 653 million (with a low population growth projection) and 904 (with a high population growth projection) in 2025. Water pollution on the other hand propagates many water borne diseases like diarrhea, hook worm, cholera, typhoid, paratyphoid etc. Moreover GREEN India Report of Tata Energy Research Institute (1997) reveals that from 1947 to 1997 availability of fresh water decreased by two thirds and area covered by soil erosion rose by in the neighborhood of 80 million hectares. On water pollution the report indicates that class one and class two cities generated around 20 billion litres of sewage wastewater per day but treated only a-tenth. The total sewage generation from urban areas increased six times in the last fifty years (1947-97). The water need of major water consuming industries like agro-based units, refineries, petrochemicals, fertilizers and chemicals had grown 40 times but these were not treating a large quantity of generated wastewater.

SOLID WASTE AND LIVESTOCK

Solid waste and hazardous wastes cause risks, which are often acute. Solid waste includes all types of solid and semi solid waste products like ashes, garbage, house sweepings etc. It enhances rat population and propagates many diseases. While dry waste is not disposed of local people burnt it in unscientific manners resulting in smoke and toxic gases in the air. Apart from that hospital waste also deteriorates health standards among city dwellers. Nursing homes, clinics, even bigger hospitals dump waste untreated. In lieu of acting as healing centre, hospitals themselves are becoming a source of disease. Moreover untreated wastes are being scattered by the birds and animals from the dumped sites, which often degrade environment. Diseases spread by rotting garbage and blocked drains are equally dangerous. Further these solid wastes create pollution of ground water resources. It has already been reported that municipal solid waste has increased seven times while the disposal of solid waste continues to be unscientific. It is estimated that generation of solid waste in major Indian cities is about 50 kgs per capita per day, while collection and disposal of such waste by the municipal corporation are almost absent.

The livestock population, however, has continued to grow in the country though not keenly. Total livestock excluding poultry increased by 32.3 per cent in India between 1961-1990. The National Family Health Survey (1992-93) reveals that household having livestock in urban areas is 14.3 per cent. The density of livestock per hectare of land clubbing together forest, agricultural land including present fallows, pastures and cultivable waste was only 1.71 per cent in 1990 in India as a whole. The growth of poultry has been more significantly than of livestock. The total number of poultry increased by 141 per cent between 1961 and 1990 in the country as a whole. Livestock pressure on land, number of mammal and bird species and also higher plant species threatened having an adverse effect on regeneration capacity is a traditional source of worry to the environmentalists and foresters in India (Table 8.2).

Table 8.2
Mammal, Bird and Higher Plant Species
Threatened Environment

	Mammal and birds species		*Higher plant species*	
	Number	*Number threatened*	*Number*	*Number threatened*
India	1,239	148	16,000	1,236
Indonesia	1,955	232	29,375	264
Kenya	1,203	67	6,506	240
Malaysia	787	76	15,500	490
South Africa	843	49	23,420	2,215
Sri Lanka	338	25	3,314	455

Source: World Bank.1999. *Entering 21st century*, World Development Report 1999/2000, Washington DC.

INDOOR AND OUTDOOR AIR POLLUTION

Air pollution has many perilous chronic hygienic impacts. The worst pollutants of air include carbon monoxide, sulphur dioxide, nitrogen oxide etc. Automobiles, industries, electric power plants and households are the main sources of air pollution. Indoor and outdoor air pollution breaks out various air borne diseases like pneumonia, bronchitis, asthma and even lung cancer along with many other problems. Vehicle emissions have been identified as the greatest environmental danger in a large number of cities in developing countries. So far as carbon dioxide emissions are concerned, in Table 8.3 country wise percentage of global carbondioxide emissions reveal that a list of 12 countries taken together contribute 62.8 per cent of total carbondioxide emissions, out of which USA alone share 23.4 per cent of world emissions. Hence, almost one-fourth of the global carbondioxide emissions come from USA alone. Besides, China and India contribute 14.9 per cent and 4.4 per cent of global carbondioxide emissions because of their high population, while their per capita emissions are only 2.8 and 1.1 metric tons respectively compared to 7 to 20 metric tons per capita emissions for rich income countries. Although the low-income countries contribute a high percentage of emission, but as far as per capita emissions are concerned, they contribute a low level as compared to rich income countries. It is interest to note that there is a link between carbondioxide emissions and average annual growth rate of GNP. Countries like China and India with a high average annual growth rate of GNP have largest share of emissions. Indonesia contributes a little percentage of emissions of 1.1 having average annual growth rate of (-) 14.8 per cent. It has further been observed that there is a far correspondence between high percentage of world GNP and percentage of world carbondioxide emission. By and large, countries having a large share in world GNP contribute larger percentage in emission. Obviously, mighty countries are definitely responsible for the emissions of carbondioxide in the atmosphere. Studies run by National Environmental Engineering Research Institute reveals that the level of pollution due to round the clock automobile emissions in Indian cities is on the rise if compared to other cities of the world. Particulate emitted by vehicles pose a hazard to health of human beings, animals and also to longevity of the property. However the damage due to particulate is rather indirect and slow but among the gaseous components, oxides of nitrogen and nitrated organic are considered to be most hazardous. Even very small quantities of these chemicals cause problems like irritation of eyes, nose and other delicate membranes of the body. While not so dreadful, carbon monoxide is also hazardous to human beings and animals. It reacts and neutralizes of a portion of the hemoglobin in the blood and thus reducing respiratory capacity.

The pollutants emitted by selective industries like cement, leather, paints, aluminium, fertilizers, sugar and paper have damaging effects on human health, cattle health, forests and biodiversity. The diseases namely asthma and chronic bronchitis, respiratory troubles, teeth and gum problems, eye and ear diseases and so on frequently attacking the people of industrial regions are attributable to the air pollution caused by industries. The health damage due to environmental pollution has been identified in many studies. Meanwhile all most all-state pollution control broads have found pollutants of selective industries and their adverse impacts on human health (Table 8.4).

Table 8.3
Country-wise Share in Global Carbondioxide Emissions and Average Annual Growth of GNP

Country	*Carbon dioxide emission (% of world)*	*Carbon dioxide emission (per capita metric tons)*	*Share in world population (%)*	*Average annual growth rate of GNP*	*Share in world GNP (%)*
USA	23.4	20	4.6	3.7	27.4
China	14.9	2.8	21	7.4	3.2
Japan	5.2	9.3	2.1	(-) 2.6	14.1
India	4.4	1.1	16.6	6.1	1.4
Germany	3.8	10.5	1.3	(-) 0.4	7.3
UK	2.5	9.5	1.0	2.0	4.3
Italy	1.8	13.7	0.5	6.1	0.4
Canada	1.8	7.0	0.9	2.3	4.0
Australia	1.4	16.7	0.3	3.8	1.1
South Africa	1.3	7.3	0.7	0.6	0.4
Brazil	1.2	1.7	2.8	0	2.6
Indonesia	1.1	1.2	3.4	(-) 14.8	0.4

Source: World Bank.1999. *Entering 21st century*, World Development Report 1999/2000, Washington DC.

Smoke and fumes resulting from indoor use of biofuels jeopardize health standards more than any other outdoor degradation. In India the most important disease associated with indoor and outdoor air pollution is probably acute respiratory infection. The acute respiratory infection among children below five years of age is 86 per cent in India and at global level it is also single largest disease category. A balance sheet of human development (1990-97) highlights that every year nearly 3 million people in the world fall prey to air pollution, out of which more than 80 per cent from indoor air pollution. An analysis of National family Health Survey data reveals that adults over 30 years living in households using biofuels had around 30 per cent more partial blindness and 170 per cent higher tuberculosis rate than those living in households using clean fuel. Estimates available from a recent study on annual premature death to children under 5 years of age and adult women are in the range of 4,10,000-7,90,000 (Table 8.5). These estimates are however only for specific diseases there are certainly on other population groups and from other disease also.

Table 8.4
Adverse Impacts of Industrial Pollution on Human Health

Industry	*Pollutants*	*Damaging impacts on human health*
Cement	Cement dust	Asthma and other bronical problems
Leather	Sulphur oxide and other acid gas	Suffocation, bronical problems
Paints	Sulphur dioxide, hydrogen sulphide and sticky suspended particulate matter	Suffocation, irritation of throat and eyes, irritation of lung, blockage of oxygen
Aluminum	Ash, acid waste and sewage water	Blood poisoning, suffocation, lung cancer, health diseases
Iron and steel	Slag, dust and sludge	Headache, corrosion of teeth, cold, eye defects, lung diseases
Fertilizer	Urea dust, ammonia, phosphate, solid waste-fly ash	Suffocation, bronchitis, edema of lungs, irritation of throat

Source: Choudhury, A and Sahu, N.C. 1999. Environmental excise duty and emission tax: a comparative analysis in the context of India. *Finance India*, XII (1): 129-130.

Table 8.5
Estimated Annual Premature Deaths from Indoor Air Pollution

(a)	*Strong evidence*	3,10,000-4,70,000
	Acute respiratory infection	Children age below 5 years
	Chronic obstructive pulmonary disease	Women
	Lung cancer from coal use	Women (few in India)
(b)	Moderate evidence	50,000-1,30,000
	Blindness	Women (no death)
	Perinatal effects	Insufficient data for estimates
	Tuberculosis	Women
(c)	Suggestive evidence	50,000-1,90,000
	Cardiovascular disease	Women
	Asthma	Women (few in India)
	Gross total of all three categories	4,10,000-7,90,000

Source: Smith, K.R.1998. *Indoor air pollution in India: national health impacts and cost effectiveness of intervention*, Report Prepared for Capacity 21 Project of India.

DATA AND METHODOLOGY

In the present endeavour three villages of Jalpaiguri district in West Bengal have been selected using multistage sampling design to study environmental impact of pollution on rural women in general and health related diseases in particular. The villages were selected to collect detailed information regarding the losses and damages due to pollution. The information was collected through a structured questionnaire and informal group discussion (participatory rural appraisal method) with the rural communities in the villages. A sample of 150 women respondents was drawn using stratified random sampling techniques. The household survey was conducted during May–June 2004. The survey was carried out at three levels, viz. household level survey including individual responses for health status, village level and health centre level survey. At the household level multi pronged approach was used to gather different types of information relating to perceive human health. Village level information was collected from the head of the village panchayat whereas health related information was collected from administrative office of the concerned health care centre.

FINDINGS

The pollution has been consistently associated with substantial burdens of ill health in developed and developing countries. The study of selected villages reveals that women and children are badly affected by pollution. It is found that most of the diseases are indoor air and water borne, such as bronchitis, tuberculosis, asthma, eye disease, adverse pregnancy outcomes, skin infection, joint pain, other respiratory diseases, diarrhea, malaria etc. Also general muscular weakness, phlegm and cough among children have been noticed in the villages. A majority of complaints are about problems regarding bronchitis and tuberculosis. It is also reported during the period of survey that eleven women admitted to the hospital due to drinking contaminated water. The women suffering from respiratory diseases and water related diseases appear to be very high. The women suffering from respiratory diseases are 11 per cent and from water related diseases are 8 per cent. Asthma was reported by 2 per cent whereas 4 per cent reported bronchitis. The reporting of symptoms and diseases were kept into account on the basis of respondent's memory recall for all the members of the households. Incidence of asthmatic symptoms noticed to be higher among women who cook inside compared to those who cook open air. An adjusted odds ratio of 2 for blindness among women was found in biomass using households. Adverse pregnancy outcomes (still birth, low birth weight) and early infant death have been linked with outdoor air pollution and passive smoking, and it is found that odds ratio in this case is 2.67. On the basis of self reported symptomatic cases of respiratory diseases cough, breathlessness, wheezing are found to be significantly higher among those living *kachcha* houses and using biofuels for cooking compared to those living *pucca* houses and using clean fuels for cooking. The records from health centre disclose that two health centres received less than 20 female patients in a day. Average number of female patients visited in a day by all the surveyed health centres together was 37 and average number of female patients treated in a month by these health centres for respiratory or water related problems was 294. The survey signifies that percentage of affected women in each household is higher because women do with entire household work with contaminated water. The average number of days sick and unable to work every woman is about 38 a year. It is found that 3 per cent of sample women are suffering from worm infection and 1.33 per cent from jaundice. Seven such women were found who have been victimized due to arsenic poisoning. Besides diarrhea and malaria are common among a few women and children in the survey villages.

ROLE OF GLOBAL ENVIRONMENT FACILITY

The content and quality of the discourse on the environment have been transformed root and branch over the last twenty years. The available scientific proof on environmental threats demands attention of the government and the public alike. Further as a result of globalization share of responsibility towards environmental organizations have already been rising. A good number of international, governmental and non-governmental organizations have already been set up with the object of funding different environmental projects and providing information in regard to existing environmental position. Among them, Global Environment Facility (GEF) is the leading one. The GEF canalizes its resources in co-financing and cooperating with other groups and private sector while a development project on biological diversity, climate change, international waters and depletion of earth's ozone layer is taken over. Although GEF provides grants to meet the additional cost incurred on a project, but it does not cover all the international financing requirements of global environmental programs. By September 1998 approximately seven years after its formation, the GEF has allotted a total of just under $ 2 billion for the same purpose. The GEF is the interim financial mechanism of both the convention of biological diversity and convention on climate change. It is presently engaged in a range of innovative projects worldwide including support for the management of protected areas, conservation programs, biomass and energy efficiency projects, solar home system and phase out programs for chlorofluorocarbons. Apart from that, the GEF is playing a crucial role in supporting a list of measures to ensure global environmental sustainability. Similarly the role of the non-government organizations (NGOs) in generating information regarding impoverished environmental condition is also remarkable. Some NGOs often contribute by providing information on the environmentally damaging activities of the country. These organizations are also important players in efforts to support best environment practices and to discourage unsustainable activities. The NGOs are also working with the industry to set up and advise standards for areas like fishing and forestry. Therefore both government and non-governmental organizations have been contributing to foster consciousness among the people to undo the threats posed by the environmental degradation.

SUMMARY

In India several regulatory statues have been initiated regarding pollution control and environmental encouragement. The rapid changing scenario exhibits that India has learned to depend more on markets and less on government to accelerate development process, the result of which has been most unfavourable. However in order to adding momentum to the development process and to implement strong environmental policies the intervention of government becomes indispensable in the present situation.

Usually two sets of policies are advocated to fall on the underlying causes of environmental degradation and both are equally essential. The first set of policy packages includes promoting education, family planning and poverty removal programs, facilitating environmental management research etc. The purpose of second set of policy packages is to fetch the positive links between development and environment. The most common among them include targeted policies to change behaviour. In second set policy packages are based on both incentives and quantitative restrictions. However the government adopts various fiscal measures taking into account incentives based policies to control degradation. Among them, use of environmental taxes is regarded as a part of an integrated policy that has become a subject of considerable interest in most of the countries. The basic facility of environmental taxes is that it can prevent and control degradation to the possible extent on the one hand and ensure availability of funds for environmental programs on the other. The government should impose environmental taxes on those inputs, which result in pollution. Apart from the environmental taxes some countries are moving towards carbon tax to fight with the green house gases or global warming. The imposition of carbon tax helps the customers to use less energy and switch over to less carbon intensive energy sources. However the introduction of environmental taxes and integration of environmental charges with the tax policy requires a set of simple rules and criteria to ease their implementation and strengthen their effectiveness.

The government often takes measures to encourage economic efficiency on both national and international levels to minimize the degree of environmental pollution, but the measures so taken are not equal to the need. The National environment policy is designed in such a manner that those policies can provide the benefits to the individual countries only, not the rest of the world. As a result the global environmental goals are not achieved at par. Therefore government must consider the implications of indigenous environmental policy decisions for other countries for successful international cooperation in environmental arena. Side by side apart from the government machinery to enforce it is inevitable to take care of growing environmental threats in regular, rational and systematic ways and consciousness to environmental concerns is to be built up among the general masses by the government.

REFERENCES

Choudhury, A and Sahu, N.C. (1999), Environmental Excise Duty and Emission Tax: A Comparative Analysis in the Context of India. *Finance India*, XII (1): 129-130.

Nadkani, M.V. (1999), Environment in Karnataka: A Status Report. *Economic and Political Weekly*, XXXIV (9): 2736.

Smith, K.R. (1998), *Indoor Air Pollution in India: National Health Impacts and Cost Effectiveness of Intervention.* Report Prepared for Capacity 21 Project of India.

World Bank (1999), *Entering 21st century*. World Development Report 1999/2000, Washington DC.

Chapter - 9

Women, Water and Welfare

INTRODUCTION

About 80 per cent of rural people in the developing countries have no access to enhanced source of water for drinking, cooking and even sanitation purposes result of which is manifest for severe upshots not only to people's well being but also to health problems, socio-economic obscurities and inequalities. No single intervention has greater overall impact upon national development and public health than does the provision for safe drinking water and proper sanitation (World Health Organization 1996). The hurt to the physical and social environment due to water pollution with ultimate result that human hygiene may be worsen, economic productivity may be turned down and pleasure satisfaction gained from any unspoiled environment often expressed as its amenity value may also be missing to the present and future human welfare.

Water pollution is a high profile health issue, which occurs while man-made substances or natural substances in huge amount enter waterways. In spite of cleaning up waterways water pollution remains a serious global dilemma with impact on health of fresh water ecosystem and human being. Meanwhile the problem of new pollutants like pesticides has combined to heavily degrade water quality in rural villages. In rural areas surface waters like rivers and ponds are not only water sources that suffer from pollution rather ground aquifers that are critical sources of both drinking and irrigation water are also affected. Once pollutants enter ground water aquifer the damage of environment can be acute and long lasting. Since ground water is basically used for drinking purpose, pollution from untreated sewage and intensive agriculture can cause serious human health problem (Shiklomanov 1997). There is sufficient proof that ground water contamination from fertilizers, pesticides and sewage in rural villages is taking place in many parts of the developing world.

As clean water is distributed unevenly with nearly 500 million of people suffering water stress and two billion people obtain less than 50 liters of water per day to meet basic drinking, cooking and sanitation need. It has been estimated that about two-third of the world population may be subject to water crisis in 2025 and 4 billion people may be unable to meet their basic need of water. Declining water supply and quality is a foremost contributing factor to improved poverty and unemployment. Besides water scarcities add health hazards and it may be marked as ill effect of water degradation on productivity (Sarkar 2005). It has already been estimated that by 2025 thirty-four countries including India will face water stress and of late about 29 countries are suffering from water shortages. It is also expecting that number of people dwelling in water scare countries will increase from 132 million in 1990 to between 653 million (with a low population growth projection) and 904 million (with a high population growth projection) in 2025.In Africa, household water use is 47 litres per person per day on average while in Asia the average is about 90 litres. In contrast, resident of United Kingdom use average 334 litres per person per day. The United States leads the world at an estimate of 578 litres per person per day (National Wildlife Federation 2002). Add to access of fresh water is not always safe. Presently 1.1 billion people are consuming water that is not clean. In developing countries more than two million people die from causes linked to the drinking of unsafe water, inadequate sanitation and associated poor hygiene and many suffer from waterborne diseases (United Nations 2002).

Though a good number of empirical attempts have been undertaken on natural resource, environment and pollution only a few studies have focused on gender, water and health related issues. Lack of gender-disaggregated data is a major issue without which argument of the issues remains theoretical and measurement of enhancement and comprehensible gender analysis are impossible. Women could potentially make better use of rural resources such as properly purified water and sewage. With adequate support their activities could be safer and more efficient than they are at present. This paper delves into present status of women in water resource management raising emerging critical issues like water pollution and health linkages. These issues have been dealt with the help of primary data collected from water pollution-affected villages in rural West Bengal.

GENDER AND WATER SUPPLY

In rural areas it is unusual for women to have equal access to water. Women take participation in household water management in such areas where clean water and drainage are not available in house. On an average, women in developing countries walk six kilometers every day to collect water, carrying the equivalent of a suitcase (United Nations 2002). The poor in rural and urban areas tolerate a disproportionate burden of non-availability of water as well as poor quality. In this settings women are typically responsible for collecting, storing and using water and for disposing of wastewater (Roark 1984) and accountable for bulk of reproductive work in the home and field. They engage in obtaining and allocating water for hygienic purpose (cleaning, washing, disposing of waste), food production (irrigation of crops, cooking) and basic consumption. Their reproductive work in household is generally unpaid and undervalued. As a result, they are underprivileged group in the society and cannot afford to pay for many basic amenities like water contributing to their continued hardship. Research has focused on an average households in rural Africa spend 26 per cent of their time for fetching water and it is generally carried out by women. Lack of accessible safe water adds to vulnerability of women and children to diseases. Girl child very often shares the responsibility of fetching water with women in the community that can affect their health and put them at risk of attack. Rural women spend huge amount of time and energy for fetching portable water, often ignoring the loss of their physical health. Studies have shown that average energy spent on water collection varies from 12 to 27 per cent. The amount of time and effort required to collect water could influence the socio-economic and health condition of rural women in many ways. In case of income generating activities, cooking, household hygiene, agriculture and childcare women are the main beneficiaries of time and energy who gain from improved water supply facilities. In addition time saved to fetch water is normally ulilised by women productively. Such save time and energy could be used dominantly for household activities such as cleaning, cooking and childcare (Ghebremedhin 1999).

WATER POLLUTION AND HEALTH EFFECT

In rural India water supply coverage and accessibility is inadequate and absence of reliable water supply has been main basis of loss of millions of women and children. Women and often their children suffer most from water crisis and poor quality. Diseases associated with dirty water kill between 5 and 12 million people a year mostly women and children (National Wildlife Federation 2002). Women bear the physical burden of fetching water and particularly vulnerable to the effect of water contamination 70-80 per cent of illness are closely associated to water contamination. Exposure to contaminated water is linked to pregnancy failures as well as infant illness and mortality. Lack of access to safe water in rural villages forces women to spend hours every day collecting water from communal tap or directly from wells and rivers which exposes them and their children to malaria and water related diseases that affect reproductive health. In developing countries women and girls spend an estimated 40 billion hours every year carrying water from distant and frequently polluted sources. Women have been reported to spend as much as 8 hours per day carrying up to 40.8 kgs of water on their heads and hips, leading to headaches, general fatigue and pain in chest, neck and waist (United Nations 2003). Over 5 million people a year die from illnesses linked to unsafe drinking water, unclean domestic environments and improper sanitation, mostly children under age 5 (Vaz *et al.* 2001). At any time over half the population in the developing world suffers from one or more of six diseases associated with water supply such as diarrhea, ascaris, dracunculiasis, hookworm, schistosomiasis and trachoma. Annual mortality rates from the most fatal of water-borne diseases are diarrhea (3.3 million), malaria (1.5 million) and schistosomiasis (3,00000). Cholera can only be reliably prevented by ensuring that all populations have access to adequate sanitation systems and safe drinking water. Unsafe water has particular high risks for children, including mortality (Lavy *et al.* 1996). Improved water and sanitation can reduce morbidity and mortality rates of some of the most serious water-borne diseases by 20-80 per cent. Reviews show a 16 per cent to 25 per cent decrease in diarrheal morbidity resulting from improved water supply; and 20 per cent reductions in mortality, and 40 per cent reduction in diarrheal disease mortality, for some age groups when water is piped into or near the household. Improved water quality accounts for a median reduction in disease prevalence of 17 per cent, while increases in quantity show a median reduction of 27 per cent. The minimum requirement for health is 20-40 liters of water per person per day located within a reasonable distance from the household, according to the World Health Organization (1996). The National Sample Survey (1999) on drinking water, sanitation and hygiene in India provides data relating to source, quality etc. of drinking water, and conditions of sanitation and hygiene of households. This data was collected in the first half of 1998. Around 50 per cent of rural households were served by a tube well/hand pump, 26 per cent by a well, and 19 per cent by tap. Only about 31 per cent of rural households reported having their source of water within their premises, the rest had to go out to fetch their drinking water. About 60 per cent did not have to go beyond 0.2 km for this. Seasonal disruption of supply was common, especially in the summer months. Households still depended on supplementary sources, especially where tube well or hand pump was the main source. Practices of filtering or boiling water before drinking were almost non-existent.

DATA AND METHODOLOGY

In the present endeavour five villages in rural West Bengal, India have been selected using multistage sampling design to study environmental impact of water pollution on rural women in general and health related diseases in particular. The villages were selected to collect detailed information regarding the losses and damages due to water pollution. The information was collected through a structured questionnaire and informal group discussion (participatory rural appraisal method) with the rural communities in the villages. A sample of 525 women respondents was drawn using stratified random sampling technique. The survey was carried out at three levels, viz. household level survey including individual responses for health status, village level and health centre level survey. At the household level multi-pronged approach was used to gather different types of information relating to perceive human health. Village level information was collected from the head of the village panchayat whereas health related information was collected from administrative office of the concerned healthcare centre.

FINDINGS

The main concentration of women in the study was in the age group of 25 to 45 and the mean age of respondents was 31.6. At the same time, 7.4 per cent of the respondents were virtually girl child. Among the respondents, 21.9 per cent were housewives and majority engaged either in informal activities like beedi rolling, agricultural work, paid domestic services, rural artisans etc. or acted as helping hands with their mother at home. The overall level of education of respondents was poor. The number of women who reported having completed middle or high school education appeared to be insignificant. Almost 5.5 per cent of the respondents reported that they completed middle or high school levels and 19.6 per cent of them had primary schooling experience. It was quite encouraging to find four graduate women too. The remainder had no education at all. The survey discloses that 75.8 per cent women were married at the time of survey and most of them had children with 0.8 on average.

The presence of divorced or separated women was relatively low.

The study examined how many of the rural households have access to tube wells or hand pumps water in the house. However, only 7.6 per cent of rural households had access to drinking water in their homes i.e. tube well while 92.4 per cent had to fetch water from a source outside their home spending an average 3 to 4 hours a day. Of these households, 41.9 per cent accessed community taps, 34.7 per cent relied on neighbour sources, which was next to their house. The remaining percentage might access more than one sources of water. Often they had to face a long queue at the tap and make 4 to 5 trips daily to meet the requirement of the family. The requirement of water of an average household was 100 to 150 litres per day depending on the members of the family. Sometimes to keep away from distance of the community tap or on account of frequent disturbances in power supply women had to use water from *kaccha* wells for drinking purpose without boiling. Apart from using tap water the households used water from hand pumps, tube wells and wells as other sources sharing with the neighbours. It is observed that majority of the women had to manage their own household task independently. The workingwomen had to combine wage work with their other responsibilities. It is found that their husbands spent a little time on the large bulk of daily indoor activities like washing clothes and utensils, water collection and cooking. Often bathing of animals was to be performed by women in village ponds or cannels where washing mouth in the morning by people is a common phenomenon. Survey reveals that young women and children took bath in nearby ponds located in the villages. Other used wells for taking bath without having any sheds. Majority (61.1 per cent) of the houses used kaccha latrine and many possessed almost an open urinal made with two bricks or stones for sitting, which was often connected with a narrowly dug sewage. The respondent women were asked to indicate the type of container they used for fetching water, 26.9 per cent used a metal container and 73.1 per cent a plastic container. The study shows that majority (68.2 per cent) of women washed domestic utensils and clothes at the nearby ponds because it saved them time and effort. If they had no household water source, they had to carry water into the house from out side wells or tube wells. For most women, those who lived in houses without a drainage system, the biggest problem was that all water used in the house had to be carried outside and thrown into the street or pond.

The pollution has been consistently associated with substantial burdens of ill health in developed and developing countries. The study of selected villages reveals that women and children were badly affected by water pollution. It is found that most of the diseases were indoor air and water borne, such as bronchitis, tuberculosis, asthma, eye disease, adverse pregnancy outcome, skin infection, joint pain, other respiratory diseases, diarrhea, malaria etc. Also general muscular weakness, phlegm and cough among children had been noticed in the villages. It is also reported during the period of survey that seventeen women admitted to the hospital due to drinking contaminated water. The women suffering from respiratory diseases and water related diseases appeared to be very high. The women suffering from respiratory diseases were 7.8 per cent and from water related diseases are 28.2 per cent. The reporting of symptoms and diseases were kept into account on the basis of respondent's memory recall for all the members of the households. Adverse pregnancy outcomes (still birth, low birth weight) and early infant death had been linked with water pollution, and it is found that odds ratio in this case was 2.3. The records from health centres in the study villages disclose that three health centres received less than 60 female patients in a day. Average number of female patients visited in a day by all the surveyed health centres together was 113 and average number of female patients treated in a month by these health centres for respiratory or water related problems was 1454. The survey signifies that percentage of affected women in each household was higher because women do with entire household work with contaminated water. The average number of days sick and unable to work every woman was about 47 a year. It is found that 8 per cent of sample women were suffering from worm infection and 4.6 per cent from jaundice. Seventy-nine such women were found who have been victimized due to arsenic poisoning. Besides diarrhea and malaria were common among few women and children in the survey villages.

SUMMARY

In rural villages underprivileged households often access clean water come across themselves even poorer as a result of ill health caused by the non-existence of safe water. Women are the crucial custodians for those who fall ill from water-related diseases, reducing their time available for education and productive economic efforts. When water supplies become contaminated or inadequate, women must spend more time and energy to find and collect safe water for their household use. The study reveals that women residing in the area without adequate clean water spent more on medical treatment and most of the poor women in the study areas work as daily labourers in the informal sector, they immediately loss wages if they are too ill to attend the job. Hence a community without sufficient water supply and proper sanitation can be exposed to several difficulties and to alleviate such problem community participation promotion may be an appropriate solution.

REFERENCES

Ghebremedhin, Y. (1999), *Effects on Insufficient Water Supply and Sanitation. Integrated Development for Water Supply and Sanitation*, Ethiopia.

Lavy, V, Strauss, J., Thomas, D., de Vreyer, P. (1996), Quality of Health Care, Survival and Health Outcomes in Ghana. *Journal of Health Economics*, 15 (3): 333-357.

National Sample Survey Organization (1999) *Drinking Water, Sanitation and Hygiene in India*. Report 449 (54/31/1), New Delhi.

National Wildlife Federation (2002), *Population, Water and Wildlife: Finding a Balance.* Washington, DC.

Roark, P.P. (1984), Women and Water. In P.G. Bourne (ed.). *Water and Sanitation: Economic and Sociological Perspective.* Academic Press, Orlando.

Sarkar, S. (2005), Natural Resource Environment, Pollution and Women Health. In T.Sabnna (ed.) *Agriculture and The WTO.* Serial Publications, New Delhi.

Shiklomanov, I.A. (1997), *Comprehensive Assessment of the Fresh Water Resources of the World: Assessment of Water Resources and Water Availability in the World.* World Meteorological Organization and Stockholm Environment Institute, Sweden.

United Nations (2002), Johannesburg Summit 2002. *Fact Sheets.* World Summit on Sustainable Development, New York.

United Nations (2003), *Global Population and Water: Access and Sustainability*. United Nations Population Fund, New York.

Vaz, L. and Jha, P. (2001), *Note on the Health Impact of Water and Sanitation Services*. CMH Working Paper Series, Paper No. WG5: 23, Commission on Macroeconomics and Health, World Health Organization, Geneva.

World Health Organization (1996), *Water and Sanitation*. Fact Sheet No. 112, Geneva.

Chapter - 10

Women, Energy and Empowerment

INTRODUCTION

More than half the world's population lives in rural areas, nearly 90 per cent of them some 2.8 billion in the developing countries. The vast majority of these people are dependent on the traditional fuels of wood, dung and crop residue, often using primitive and inefficient technologies. For many, this combination barely allows fulfillment of the basic human needs of nutrition, warmth and light, let alone the possibility of harnessing energy for productive uses which might begin to permit escape from the cycle of poverty. Demographic trends risk exacerbating the situation. Most of today's 2 billion people without adequate energy services are in rural areas, but urban populations are projected to grow more rapidly. Far from easing rural energy-poverty, this is likely to reinforce policy makers' preoccupation with urban issues, while increasing competition for rural energy supplies. It is calculated that an amount of energy roughly equivalent to 7 per cent of the world's electricity production today could cover basic human needs. In an age of apparently advanced technological and management skills, we have failed in this relatively modest challenge. Dependence on traditional fuels will long remain a reality, given its level (reaching over 95 per cent in some countries). It is not so much their use that is wrong, as the manner in which they are being managed and used, not always at a sustainable rate. Inefficient technologies and appliances mean that precious wood fuel resources are wasted and high indoor smoke pollution severely impairs health. The burden of this traditional energy use falls disproportionately on women. Gradually a transition to modern energy systems (which may utilise traditional energy sources) must be achieved if sustainable economic activity is to be realised in rural areas. As much traditional energy use occurs outside the market sector, data on it is geographically inconsistent and discontinuous. This statistical invisibility of much rural energy use reinforces its neglect and hampers the development of effective policy. In addition, the enormous variety of energy use patterns, even within quite short distances, makes extrapolation dangerous. While precision is difficult most energy in rural areas is used for residential purposes, predominantly for cooking. Energy in itself may not be a basic human need, but it is critical to the alleviation of starvation. Staple foods, on which poor people depend, are often inedible when raw and energy is needed for food production and preservation. In cold climates it is also essential for adequate warmth. As incomes rise above subsistence levels, energy for lighting, refrigeration and productive activities (especially agriculture) brings new possibilities for education, health and other community services as well as income enhancement. Even small quantities can be critical to breaking the poverty cycle. At least initially, gross energy consumption may actually decline as more efficient, modern energy technologies are introduced, before a broader range of energy applications takes it higher. For example, for equivalent light output, kerosene lamps are much more energy-intensive than electric lighting (World Energy Council 1999).

ENERGY-INFORMALITY

In the developing economies a substantial share of employment is indeed in informal category and women in all age groups depend on the informal sector more heavily than men. Women are over represented in this sector in the sense that their share in the sector is higher than their share in total labour force. Most women tend to be own account workers and only a few are heads of micro enterprises. Relatively lower level of education among women, compared to men, seems to explain, in part, this gender differential in informal employment. Discrimination in the labour market also explains in part the disproportionate concentration as it limits women's access to formal and wage employment. Women also face additional constraints because of their homemaking and childcare responsibilities, which limits their participation in formal employment. Even within the informal sector more women than men seem to be in poor quality employment. In Latin America more women seem to be in the unpaid categories than men. In Africa the proportion of unpaid workers working in family owned enterprises among women appears to be relatively high compared to other regions. The causes for participation in the informal sector can be economic and non-economic. Economic reasons are related to unemployment and an inflexible formal labour market, a declining real price of capital and the high cost of formal production. Besides, non-economic causes are concerned with a greater flexibility and satisfaction in work, a complete use of workers professional qualifications and increased leisure time. There are two groups of factors, which determine the decision to become active in the informal sector, more specifically, the structural as well as opportunity factors.

The structural factors consist of financial pressure, socio-psychological pressure and institutional constraints. The opportunity factors consist of individual background, skills, education, living condition or non-individual components, environment, values, standards etc. (Sarkar 2004). Unlike modern fuels, the supply of biofuels such as wood and charcoal are still largely uncontrolled and based in the informal sector. Rural populations generally supply themselves from surrounding forests and from trees in the landscape, in most cases in quantities that do not exceed sustainability limits. The supply of biomass fuel for the cities is also uncontrolled and in most cases, biomass production is unsustainable. Wood is felled in state-owned forests by dealers, but the cost of replacing the trees is not paid, with the result that forests are deteriorating rapidly around major cities. Past efforts to relieve the resulting firewood shortage by encouraging farmers to grow trees have largely failed because the costs of this far exceed the short term costs of gathering fuel from existing forests (French 1986). However new efforts to empower local communities to manage the forests in their areas in a sustainable way for the production, among other things, of biomass fuels are encouraging, particularly as this could provide income sources for the poor within the community. In most developing countries the majority of informal sector enterprises are owned and operated by women, with women making up the largest proportion of the work force. Despite this, the contribution of women entrepreneurs to national economies is not explicit in national statistics, leading to the development of policies that do not deal with the specific barriers faced by women linked to their gender-defined roles. Their enterprises tend to be concentrated in a relatively narrow range of activities such as beer brewing, knitting, dressmaking, crocheting, cane work and retail trading. These activities tend to have disproportionately low rates of return compared to the activities undertaken by men. However despite the low financial returns, women's enterprises provide important sources of household income, even in male-headed households. Women headed enterprises are frequently located in the home and these cottage industries tend to be overlooked by agencies because they are in the informal sector, which is diffuse and difficult to reach. When women are forced to close their enterprises, it is often for non-business reasons and linked to factors associated with working from home. The low rates of return prevent inward investment, hindering innovation and expansion, which are regarded as key factors in enterprise sustainability (Grosh and Somolekae 1996). There is little research to explain what forces drive these startups and shutdowns, and how gender influences these processes. Women's access to resources (such as credit, land and education, which are recognised as key factors in micro enterprise development) is significantly less than that of men. Generally, research in small and medium-scale enterprise sustainability indicates that a lack of working capital is one of the two most common causes of enterprise failure (Grosh and Somolekae 1996). Women's access to decision-making within the household and community is also restricted, reducing their ability to influence processes and resource allocation. Given the disproportionate number of poor women in rural areas, research which takes into account gender aspects of the transformation of structures and processes could make a significant contribution to the development of gender equitable sustainable livelihoods. The role of energy in the sustainability of women's enterprises is also not well understood. In food processing enterprises it has been estimated that energy costs are 20 to 25 per cent of the total inputs, which would suggest that technological interventions could increase the scale and profitability of these businesses. The types of enterprises that women are traditionally involved in are energy intensive and rely on biomass fuels. Even in rural areas, women may have to buy fuel wood to run enterprises such as beer making (McCall 2001). An important issue is what sort of mechanisms can assist women in gaining access to improved energy services. Grain mills, which are very popular with women, since they improve product quality as well as reducing women's labour, are typically only provided by the private sector, and are still absent in many rural locations. A much more systematic approach is needed, possibly with some form of incentive to encourage the spread of mills to areas not yet served. A general rule that can be learnt from attempts to introduce technology for women is that if it does not reduce the labour in household tasks then, no matter how beneficial the technology, it is likely to have low acceptance. There are positive examples of women taking up energy technologies that have contributed to increasing their incomes. It is found that women's groups in Ghana use LPG for fish preservation, giving them a better quality product than when using wood, and enabling them to reach export standards, considerably improving their income (Mensah 2001). Women may in fact be best entrants to become energy entrepreneurs. It has indicated that improved stove programmes in India run by women tend to be rather successful because they are able to more easily approach their clients (Sarin 1984). However energy entrepreneurship could extend beyond stoves to include energy services, for example the supply of and even the repair of, modern energy appliances such as solar panels. There is an enormous need for agents in rural areas who can distribute such equipment on a viable basis, notwithstanding with some support in the short term. Women who live in rural areas know and understand local circumstances and needs and may have a much clearer idea about the energy services that rural people desire.

In addition a woman may be able to sell more effectively to other women, since access to female clients is not hindered by social constraints. This may in fact be the best route to greater women's participation in household energy choice.

Poor rural people struggle for energy for cooking. Biomass fuel accounts for 76.3 per cent of the total fuel in rural industries such as paddy parboiling, smithies, potteries etc. (Eusuf 1997) and is the common fuel for the domestic rural sector. Wood fuel has become scarce over the last few years through deforestation. Its share as a percentage of total biomass fuel had decreased from 63 per cent in 1981 to 22 per cent in 1990 (Douglas 1981). Biofuels can damage people's health, because they give off smoke that contains many hazardous particles. Studies of rural areas show that smoke levels inside dwellings often far exceed safe levels recommended by the World Health Organization (2000). Cooking with biofuels does not cause health problems everywhere, but in houses that have poor ventilation it can be as dangerous as smoking cigarettes. A study in Gambia, for example, examined the health of 500 children under five years old. It found that children who were carried on their mothers' backs as they cooked in smoky huts were six times more likely to develop acute respiratory illness than other children. Studies of women in Nepal and India exposed to biomass smoke but who did not smoke themselves found that their death rate from chronic respiratory disease was similar to that of male heavy smokers. The use of biofuels can also damage the environment. The search for fuel wood often involves chopping down local trees. Higher income countries also depend much less on biofuels than do poor countries. The best schemes for improving rural energy may therefore fail if other policies prevent economic growth. An important aspect of this involved looking at women's work and its significance for total production, a perspective that raised the question of energy sources, including the energy expenditure of women labour. It has also led to a broader shift in thinking about energy with linkages to women's gestured position and reduction of poverty, for example, economic and political linkages, which ranged from inappropriate pricing policies and subsidies for the fuel. In these emerging perspectives, it was noted that from the perspective of the rural women, the energy crisis was a fuel wood crisis; the dependence of large sections of the world's population on hitherto unexamined forms of biomass energy was pointed out, and it was noted that for many, deforestation had meant that in some cases it was more difficult to cook the food than to grow it. In spite of these merging perspectives the dominant paradigm continues to observe energy as large-scale, capital intensive technological projects run by professional experts, which ignores the actual definition of energy as the capacity for doing work and overcoming resistance.

ENERGY-EMPOWERMENT LINKAGES

It is imperative to look into the linkages of energy and empowerment of women in the area of the opportunity cost (that is alternative income earned) of women's labour time saved by the energy projects. Whether or not a farm household seeks greater efficiency in fuel use (an improvement which will cost some money) depends on the opportunity cost of labour in biofuel collection and cooking. The lower the income or production lost by women spending more time in collecting, the less will be the incentive to adopt improved stoves, or to switch to more efficient commercial fuel. If employment or self-employment were available, it would be preferable to earn cash as a worker and buy biofuel than collect it. If women's possible labour time saved by improved stoves has no alternative income-earning possibilities, even if women were the household decision-makers, they would not make a decision in favour of spending cash to acquire improved stoves. The effect of women's unvalued labour time holds good even with respect to labour of children (girls, in particular). To the extent that the education of girls is not valued (because they will go away after marriage and the investment in their education will be 3 lost to their parental families), there will be no pressure to economies on the labour of girls, who also do part of the labour of biofuel collection and cooking. The needs of domestic or reproductive labour are the least addressed in energy development. In the market-dominated system, the extent to which reducing the drudgery of domestic labour and its health hazards are dealt with depends on the extent to which women's work is monetized. It also requires attention to what are now 'women's needs' in the existing division of labour. For instance, changes in house or kitchen design to promote more gender-equal roles (sharing of domestic labour between women and men) and to make the labour less hazardous need to be integrated into new architectural practices. But this requires both more women as architects and energy experts and consultation with women user of energy systems, so that they can participate in their design, and changes in gender relations, which makes these energy changes necessary. Can energy play a leading role in stimulating these changes? It is not energy itself that has certain inevitable consequences, but the economic and social situation in which technologies are introduced, and the balance of forces at any time. Certainly systems of cooking, house cleaning, house washing etc. which reduce the labour in these activities, may make it easier for working couples to share domestic duties. But it is also possible for such energy uses not to inevitably lead to such changes in sharing. Japan is a good example of all the available energy uses not leading to any sharing of housework between the two genders. So long as women do not insist that their careers are not subsidiary to those of their husbands, and that housework be shared or socialized (even commercialized in parts, like laundry washing of garments, or preparation of meals), there need not be any change in gender relations, no matter what energy is available. Feminists have long argued that the family cannot be seen as a philanthropic institution in which the welfare of all is uniformly the principle of distribution of labour and benefits. Supplementing the gender inequalities are the age-based hierarchies, which both extends/reproduces nurturance as well as oppression. The family is not a sacrosanct institution inside which the law cannot reach. In fact, one of the advances of the feminist debate of the last few decades is to extend the notion of human rights from merely regulating relations between the state and individuals to one between individuals within and across families, in a famous slogan 'the personal is political'. And the family also needs to be reformed, both in relations between the genders and in relations between the generations.

WOMEN, ENERGY AND DEVELOPMENT

Most of the few women working in the energy sector do not address gender aspects. This may be due to the fact that women in extreme minority positions in their professional work are subject to an enormous pressure to adaptation. Usually, they are struggling to be acknowledged as experts, and thus frequently outdistance themselves from other women. To take on the position of the "disadvantaged" in this situation and this is how women are seen in terms of women promotion and women approaches would mean to risk the hard won acceptance of their expert reputation. Even the few women who oppose to the pressure to adaptation and do concern themselves with gender aspects do not "mainstream" these aspects, but often address them in the frame of volunteer work or private initiatives, separate from the 'real' energy policy and energy planning within their professional work. As a consequence, there is a complete lack of gender mainstreaming in the sense of screening of all politics to their different impacts on women and men. As a sphere related to technology, energy is a highly male dominated issue. Given the fact that women routinely work a few hours more per day that men in most regions of the world. The importance of increasing women's leisure time has been noteworthy. Importantly, leisure is not a function enjoyment, but a function of self-development, and thereby a function of production and empowerment too. But then the factor of the gendered control of household income comes into the picture. The key decision- maker in the household does not treat the leisure or labour time of all its members equally. The leisure time of the men and boys is viewed more favourably than the leisure time of women and girls. It is a common knowledge that women in rural Asia routinely wake up an hour before men and go to sleep an hour after men. Further, they do not have much time to rest in between, while men usually rest when they return from the fields. In a village of Hani people in Yunnan, China, it has been noticed that money was spent on acquiring cassette players (with which men could listen to music in their substantial leisure time) rather than on getting piped water or improved stoves, both of which would have reduced women's working hours. Similar reports came from the villages of Punjab, in India. What this means is that in any process of empowerment, anticipation of leisure time and expectation of enjoyment on the part of women have to be continually cultivated, the more so because self-sacrifice and denial of pleasure have been important part of their cultural socialization. How do the inequalities of power, between North and the South, between States and groups affect the flow information and cultural exchanges in the new energy paradigm? More of the information and cultural features will flow from those who are more powerful. But this predominance is due not only to power but also to the acceptance of the values of the powerful as those, which are valid for the whole world and represent the future of all peoples. The market process/ economic and technological globalization takes place in a social-cultural context where there is substantial inequality of ownership of assets/ property and a lack of agreed criteria of distribution justice that provide a basis on which property and capability redistribution could be considered. It is necessary to consider the empowerment implication of property ownership and to consider whether the asset titles that have led to existing inequalities are responsible for social and institutional exclusion of women, and very much so in energy institutions. Given South Asia's shared cultural history of classic patriarchy and specific forms of violence against women, it is not possible to give priority to cultural ethos of have a programme for change that concentrates on values. It is misleading for the social scientists and planners to regard values as the foundation of a society. Also, there is flattening out of the antagonism between culture and economy. Cultural forms and practices no longer stand apart from economic reality of energy structures and call it into a question, notably, in relation to travel and tourism the impact of informational society for instance, call centers in India, or the garment industry in Bangladesh. Cultural relativism arguments cannot be used to defend inequality. A discriminatory practice, however, culturally entrenched, has to be ended. A long history of discrimination does not justify the existence (e.g. slavery, untouchability, prostitution). Substantive equality also happens to be essential to the economic and social prosperity of a country. By denying itself energy and intellect of half of the population, a discriminatory society stifles its own economic and social growth and condemns itself to continued under development, as noted in reports from Indonesia and other countries in Asia and Africa. Social and institutional inclusion of women is pivotal to the context of empowerment and crucial for a sustainable development of energy.

SUMMARY

Women and their opinions have long been overlooked in the process of development. In the use of energy technologies too, their role has been either minimized or totally neglected in the policy formulation as well as project design despite the fact that women are the primary users of energy at the household level. Poor households have to adopt few strategies to accommodate the impact of increased direct and indirect energy costs on their already limited household budget. Firstly, they have to change the type of energy they use, switching to cheaper options. This will involve a shift down the energy ladder. Secondly, poor households have to reduce their overall consumption of energy in a variety of ways such as reducing the number of meals cooked per day , switching over to cheaper, usually less nutritious, food and in extreme cases reduced the amount of food consumed etc. and finally, the poor have to cut down their expenditure on non-energy goods. Access to energy options should be promoted through setting up distribution channels that are nearer to the users. In addition to this, financing mechanisms that promote access to energy services for the rural and urban poor should have strategies to address the needs of women and poor men who are in most cases excluded from such initiatives. Such access to energy services can enable women to get into income earning activities that will not only benefit them but also the members of their households, including support to the income earned by the male spouse. Strategies to enable women to participate in decision-making should be promoted, especially in cases where energy policy planning and implementation of programmes are being undertaken. The demand for energy services is influenced by decisions made on the use of the service, who uses it and who will benefit. Women and men have different needs and uses of energy due to the differences in the tasks they undertake in both the household and workplaces. Decisions on household expenditure within the available resources therefore tend to favour the demands of men and male children due to the patriarchal set-up of decision-making. Headship of household also plays a role here, since in those households where women manage the household income they are able to decide and make acquisition of energy services a priority concern. Access to energy is therefore hindered by the decisions of the users and the benefit envisaged.

REFERENCES

Eusuf, M. (1997), *Dissemination of Biogas Technology in Bangladesh*. Paper Presented at the National Seminar on Renewable Energy for Poverty Alleviation (NSREPA-97). Institute of Engineers, Bangladesh.

Douglas, J. (1981), *Supply and Demand of Forest Products and Future Development Strategies: Consumption and Supply of Wood and Bamboo in Bangladesh*. Field Document 2, FAO/ UNDP/ BDG/78/010.

French, D. (1986), Confronting an Unsolvable Problem: Deforestation in Malawi. *World Development*, 14 (4): 531-540.

Grosh, B. and Somolekae, G. (1996), Mighty Oaks from Little Acorns: Can Micro Enterprise Serve as the Seedbed of Industrialization? *World Development*, 24 (12): 1879-1890.

McCall, M.2001. Brewing Rural Beer Should be a Hotter Issue. *Boiling Point*, 47: 23-25.

Menash, S.A. (2001), Energy for Rural Women's Enterprises. In *Generating Opportunities: Case Studies on Energy and Women*. United Nations Development Programme, New York.

Sarin, M. (1984), *Nada Chula: A Handbook*. Voluntary Health Association of India, Delhi.

Sarkar, S. (2004), Theorising in Informal Sector: Concept and Context. *Social Action*, 54 (40): 359-373.

World Energy Council (1999), *The Challenge of Rural Energy Poverty in Developing Countries*. United Nations.

World Health Organization (2000), *Addressing the Links between Indoor Air Pollution, Household Energy and Human Health.* Geneva.

Index